D1523249

THIS IS
REALLY
US

WHAT THE HIT TV SHOW
TEACHES US ABOUT
FAITH, HOPE AND LIFE

Michelle S. Lazurek

To the Pop Culture Enthusiast

God is speaking through your TV set.

Listen and obey.

Acknowledgements

As someone who watched many hours of television as a kid, I find it fitting that God would now ask me to interact with that same TV set from a new perspective—one of renewal, reconciliation and hope. As the new season of television is upon us, I can't help but notice at least three of the new TV dramas are highly spiritual in nature. While the characters quote bible verses and use social media platforms, their message is still the same: The world is hungry to fill the void that lies deep within its heart. As Christians we need to dig deep into Scripture, read between the lines, and apply Scripture in a way that points them to the only One who can quench the thirst of a dehydrated world. My hope is this book will start the conversation on how to do this.

To my husband Joe, and my kids Caleb and Leah, you still remain the three best things that have ever entered my crazy world.

To Steve Hutson, my agent and advocate. Thank you for trying to see where this would go. The lives this book touches will certainly be to your credit as much as they are to mine and to God's.

To God, my Daddy and my friend. Thank you for loving me, but more importantly, liking me. Thank you for redeeming all those years of television watching and allowing me to be a voice in people's lives. Do what you will with this, as always.

Table of Contents

Chapter One
Is This Really Us

On September 20, 2016, viewers tuned in to a new drama called *This Is Us*, a seemingly mundane drama about five characters in different stages of life. By the show's end, viewers learn the characters' lives intersect in unpredictable ways again. After the first episode, audiences were buzzing with joy about the superb storytelling, relatability of the characters, and unique plot twists.

But this show is more than just any drama. The show asks an important question to both Christians and non-Christians alike: Is this really *us*?

We find appeal in the show's characters as they struggle with various aspects of life. Yet, so many Christians struggle with these same aspects and more. They struggle to find answers to life's biggest questions such as: *Why am I here?*

Where is God in all of this?

Does God see me?

From the first episode, there is a hint to the answer to some of these questions. From the first scene, director Dan Fogelman tells us a story. From the moment we join these characters in their story, we are told that this is our story, and that our lives intersect in ways unbeknownst to us. Yet, when our lives intersect, they do so in ways that touch our lives so deeply, we don't know what we would do without them. This in itself indicates to the viewer that this show has a greater purpose. We were born to connect with others.

This Is Us provides us with people with whom to journey through life, even if they mess it up from time to time. That's why this show is resonating with Christians and non-Christians everywhere. It's a living version of the Bible we read and know in our hearts. It's a story of ordinary people, like you and me, who are trying to get through life with some semblance of meaning and purpose. The story of the Pearson family is the story of you and me, and Peter and John and Paul and the woman at the well and everyone else that claims a spot in one of the most revered books in our history. This show will be remembered as one of the best in NBC's network's history as the show's characters worm their way into our heads and, ultimately, our hearts. From its skyrocketing popularity, I suspect they already have.

The Story

The main storyline is a story common to most people. A married couple, Jack and Rebecca Pearson, are about to embark on the journey toward parenthood as Rebecca goes into labor with triplets. We are also introduced to three other characters. Kate, a food addict, wrestles with her addiction to food. In her first scene, we watched as she opened her fridge to see notes to herself on all of the junk food in the fridge. Words like "this is bad," "throw this crap out," and "don't you dare eat your cake before your birthday" greet her as she fights the temptation to binge eat.

Kevin, a famous actor, is most noted for his role as "The Manny," the main character on a silly sitcom that focuses more on his bulging biceps than on its content. Kevin struggles with whether or not the world sees him as mere eye candy or as someone who is a serious actor who is engaging in meaningful work. As we watch Kevin tape an episode of "The Manny," we see the audience whistle and make catcalls at him as he, shirtless, talks to the baby he is watching.

"Do you want me to breastfeed you? Is that what you want me to do?" he says to the baby he cradles in his arms. Later, in an emotional scene with his on screen dad, his heart-wrenching monologue to his dad ends the scene with an eruption of applause. With a glimmer of hope, Kevin believes he really is being taken seriously until the director asks him to reshoot a lighter version of the scene "with the shirt off." This causes Kevin to self-destruct into a dizzying tirade, spouting derogatory comments to the audience, the director, and everyone he sets his eyes on before quitting and leaving the show abruptly.

Randall, a successful weather commodities trader, has everything he could ever dream of: a beautiful family fancy car and all the money in the world. He's still left wanting the approval of his father. In a heart-wrenching scene, Randall goes to his biological father's home and delivers a message to him that he has wanted to say his whole life.

He says to William, "My name is Randall Pearson. I'm your biological son. I'm 36 years old. Thirty-six years ago you left me at the door of the fire station. Don't worry. I'm not here because I want anything from you because I was raised by two incredible parents and have a wonderful family of my own. The car you see parked out in front of your house cost $143,000, and I bought it for cash. I Bought it for cash because I felt like it and because I can do stuff like that. You see, I've turned out pretty all right, which might surprise a lot of folks considering the fact that thirty-six years ago my life started with you leaving me on a fire station doorstep with nothing more than a ratty blanket and a crap-filled diaper. I came here today so I can look you in the eye, say that to you, and then get back in my fancy car and prove to myself and to you and to my family who loves me that I didn't need anything from you even after I knew you were."

In that moment, the audience believes that Randall can handle everything on his own. It is his self-sufficiency that is enough for him to live his life apart from his father. However, his father replies, "You want to come in?" And, surprisingly, Randall quickly says okay.

It's in this moment, we see Randall is just as broken as every other character we've seen so far. Although each character has chosen a different career path, has their own struggles, and seems to be living a separate life from the others, the audience understands that their lives intersect in more ways than one. This is made most clear to us at the very end scene when we see Jack the father catching a glimpse of his newborn babies for the first time. As Jack reflects on his three beautiful children and the overwhelming journey on which he's about to embark, a fireman comes up next to him. Making casual conversation, Jack asks the man, "Which one's yours?"

The fireman says, "None of them. Strangest thing, that baby over there was left on the doorstep of the fire station. Seems like destiny." The camera pans out to the smoking people in the waiting room and their 70s attire, and the audience quickly realizes that Kate, Kevin, and Randall are siblings, and the scenes with Jack and Rebecca depict not just any birth but Kevin's, Kate's, and Randall's births.

Dan Fogelman, director and producer of the show, skillfully interweaves two timelines: one in the late 70s when Jack and Rebecca first give birth to their children and in present day when Kevin, Kate, and Randall, now in their mid-30s, struggle with the same life issues their parents did at their age. This resonates with the audience in a way to pull on the heartstrings and makes them emotionally invested in the characters. It speaks to our hearts' deepest desire to know that life is not merely coincidence and that everything happens for reason. A plot twist like this also leaves us with more questions than answers, which leaves us wanting more by the end of the episode.

The Story Behind the Story

Introspective shows like these are not new for television.

In the 1960s and 1970s, TV was used as an escape from real life. No one expected to become a flying nun like Sally Field or be kept in a bottle to be summoned to grant every one of her master's wishes like Barbara Eden on *I Dream of Jeannie*. But as the young hippies began to grow up, get jobs and start families, they demanded something different—stories about other real life people going through the same issues as they were. The 1980s explored this type of programming with shoes such as *Thirtysomething*, another seemingly mundane drama about a group of men and women in their 30s trying to figure out life's biggest issues.

As the demand for more programs featuring real people grew, the more the networks gave in to the demand. Soon the proliferation of real life dramas and comedies emerged. The 1980s also saw a rise in women becoming strong female leads, like as shown in *Cagney and Lacey*, *Murder She Wrote,* and *Murphy Brown*. No longer were women depicted as housewives who fluffed pillows all day or those tugging at the pearls strung around their necks. Instead, programs depicted women with careers, hopes, and dreams, struggling to make ends meet day to day just like everyone else.

With the success of *The Cosby Show* and *Family Ties*, viewers got used to seeing strong male and female characters hold down successful careers and rear families.

Jack and Rebecca Pierson are the Stephen and Elise Keatons and the Cliff and Claire Huxtables of our age, but this time with some flaws. Rebecca, wracked with insecurity about being a mother, strives to prepare the perfect cranberry sauce for Thanksgiving and tells Jack, "Good is not good enough, Jack. It has to be perfect or else my sister's sweet potato pie will be perfect, and I don't want to hear my mother's passive aggressiveness if the sauce is not one hundred percent perfect." She places three locks on the inside door of their secluded cabin to keep all the bad things out. She also struggles to find her place in the singing world again after taking an eight-year hiatus.

Jack has dreams of his own, too. However, he has to put his company, Big Three Homes, on hold by taking a desk job so he can provide for his family.

Viewers are enamored with these characters because it's slightly comforting to see not everyone has it all together, even if our social media polished worlds say we do.

This Is Us is the collective sigh of relief we've all been waiting for. It's the show we as a society have not wanted but rather needed even when we didn't know we needed it. It gives the world permission to say, "I don't have it together, but it's okay because they don't either."

It's the assurance that no matter how perfect a parent we are, our kids, who live in a fallen world, will still have insecurities and addictions and pain they still have to process on their own.

The show is also unique in that we get a glimpse of what it's like to be an overweight woman in a society obsessed with weight. We get a glimpse of what it's like to live in an overweight person's world. We also get to know what it's like to live in a black person's world. Randall, no matter how successful he is in life, will always be the suspicious black man in an unfamiliar neighborhood. No other show even attempts this as skillfully as Fogelman does. This show is a unique perspective into ordinary lives of people who may share the same struggles but not as perfect as we think they are.

Russell Moore, author of the Washington post article, "Why We're Obsessed with the Hit Show *This is Us*," says:

> "This rings true because we all tend to see our lives as narrative and, like the characters in this series, the narrative is often murkier than we would like. Some of us had relatively idyllic childhoods. Some of us grew up in the specter of violence or addiction or abuse or some other awful reality. Some of us grew up wondering, as we do as we see some of the secrets of the back stories of this series unfold, whether the family figures of our past are heroes or villains or a mixture of the two. The switching back and forth between the 1980s and 2016 reminds us

that the narrative of our lives is not a straight line. Our childhoods aren't just "back there," but they intrude on our lives now, sometimes in picking at old scars and sometimes in reminding us of the small mercies that have brought us safe thus far. We wouldn't be who we are if not for the stories that have made us — stories we love, stories we hate, and sometimes stories we long to peer into but leave us in mystery."[1]

Jennifer Dukes Lee, bestselling author and fan of *This is Us*, wrote a blog post about why this show has garnered such acclaim: "*This is Us* gives us faith in humanity again. It reminds us that we belong to each other. It fills us with delight at a time when the world seems to be drowning in peril. It reminds us that we are all broken and whole – capable of laughing and crying in the same hour, or even the same minute. *This Is Us* works because this is us. It works because we are them."[2]

This is really us, indeed.

---

[1] Moore, Russell. "Why We're Obsessed with the Hit Show This Is Us." WashingtonPost.com November 30, 2016 https://wapo.st/2ycJT9t

[2] Dukes Lee, Jennifer. "The TV Show That is Saving My Sanity and Recovering My Delight." http://bit.ly/2P8NOLQ

So at first, I was thinking you know, maybe up here was that guy's part of the painting, and maybe over here was that guy's part of the painting. Then I started to think maybe we're all in the painting everywhere. I mean, before we were born, and after we die, and these colors that we keep adding, maybe they just keep adding one on top of another until eventually we're not even different colors anymore; we're just one thing. One painting.

Kevin

Chapter Two
How Does the Bible and
Pop Culture Intersect?

When I was a girl, I was content with my faith. Growing up in a Catholic home, I went to church and school, taking my beliefs for granted. It wasn't until high school when I began to question the beliefs that I held so dear. I wanted more from my faith. Instead of throwing up rote prayers when I got in a jam, I wanted to interact with God. I wanted the personal relationship a friend from work had just acquired.

Despite growing up in a home that was not devoutly religious, my friend's knowledge of Scripture was undeniable and cut to my heart. I couldn't believe that someone who had almost no religious background could know God so intimately; yet, I had attended church all my life and had only a superficial relationship. I could lie to the co-worker about having a deeper relationship than I had, but I couldn't lie to myself. I knew deep down I needed to experience God's presence in order to achieve the intimacy I desperately craved.

This is Us, in a way, is like that. It's the experience we all want from our families but never received. The Pearsons encapsulate everything in a family—bonding, two parents that love each other, families that spend time with each other. It's the experience of a family, even if we've never had that as our family.

The Bible is that same spiritual experience. The Bible is a love letter, an interaction with a living God who speaks through its pages. Reading the Bible fulfills that experience I wanted as a child. But it wasn't always that way.

For years, I just went through the motions of reading the Word, reading it to check it off a to-do list instead of interacting with it, asking the Lord to speak instead of believing he had already spoken. When I became a writer, however, all that changed.

I had to just not read the Word but study it. I had to consult with what other experts in the field had to say and interpret Scripture in a new way. Above all, I had to be still in God's presence and ask that He reveal something new in His Word to me that He had never revealed before. When that happened for the first time, it was euphoric. As I practiced this more frequently and it became a habit, I began to become in tune with the Holy Spirit. He opened my eyes to the places and ways in which God spoke to me. As I put myself in the position to interact with God, He met me right where I was.

I think this is why television and movies are such popular subjects to discuss. It's one of my favorite subjects to talk about with my friends and to read about online. That's the purpose of this book.

Christians often find it difficult to engage with the world on these issues. We feel we're *in* the world but not *of* the world (John 17:16). I think what we see on TV and in the movies is not only a reflection of our ever-changing culture but is also an opportunity to apply a never-changing word to an ever-changing world. The statistics are clear: Millennials are leaving the church.

In an article from CNN titled "Millennials leaving the church in droves, the study finds:

> Religion editor Daniel Burke confirms what church leaders have known for a long time: "Released Tuesday, the survey of 35,000 American adults shows the Christian percentage of the population dropping precipitously, to 70.6%. In 2007, the last time Pew conducted a similar survey, 78.4% of American adults called themselves Christian. In the meantime, almost every major branch of Christianity in the United States has lost a significant number of members, Pew found, mainly because Millennials are leaving the fold. More than one-third of Millennials now say they are unaffiliated with any faith, up 10 percentage points since 2007. Looking at the long view, the generational spans are striking. Whereas 85% of the silent generation (born 1928-1945) call themselves Christians, just 56% of today's younger Millennials (born 1990-1996) do the same, even though the vast majority—about eight in 10—were raised in religious homes. Each successive generation of

Americans includes fewer Christians, Pew has found."[1]

We have to interact with culture in ways that make Millennials sit up and listen. No longer can we continue doing church the way we always have. This means understanding the issues that concern the world and giving the biblical answer that a world craving for.
Author Kevin Harvey says,

As that block of ice (representing the Bible) melts, of course, it's going to flow through and cover more of the skinnier areas of the pyramid at its zenith. In the middle ages, the bible and religion was the culture and what most of the laws, traditions and opinions were built around. When trade and literacy began evolving more quickly at the end of the middle ages, due in part to the invention of the printing press, the Bible became widely available to the people than it ever had before... But still, the ice kept melting and slowly creeping down the pyramid. It certainly did not cover as much as it did at the top, but its downward flow could not be stopped. Even today, as wide as that pyramid is, the ice kept melting and seeing through the cracks, weaving its way down the cultural pyramid. As cable channels multiply, new movie studio s pop up, more and more books hit the Kindle shelves, and celebrities are made on YouTube, there's a great deal more of the pyramid to cover, and yet the water continues to find its way through more of it than you realize. You only need to know

---

[1] Burke, Daniel. "Millennials Leaving Church in Droves, Study Finds." Cable News Network https://cnn.it/2NmDwWO

what to look for." "From Legos' to Lost, Miley to the Mindy Project, Superman to Sheldon Cooper, and is a great deal more, today's pop culture is still allowing the thirst-quenching bible to seep its way in to the cracks of its foundation. Clearly, culture still finds the Bible extremely relevant, even if some don't even recognize how God's word helped shape their art. Pop culture has begun the dialogue; will the church continue it?" [2]

Where the church gets stuck is how to engage. When Christians aren't studying the Word nor allowing it to transform their souls, it's easy to simply wag a finger and think if we just stop the behavior, the heart will follow. A heart unencumbered and set free by Christ suddenly leaves room for the Holy Spirit to do His job of convicting His children. The church can demonstrate Jesus in all of its purity by interacting with culture in a way that points people to the Father.

My prayer is that as you read this book, you can see the parallels not only between the people on the TV show and in the Bible but also the people living in our world today. Perhaps you live next to a woman at the well, looking for love in all the wrong places and has a reputation to show for it. Maybe you sit next to an apostle Peter, quick to say and do the wrong thing but with a heart and a willingness to follow Jesus. Maybe there is a powerful man like Solomon, who has the world at his fingertips but secretly believes all of his life is meaningless.

---

[2] Harvey, Kevin. *All You Want to Know about the Bible and Pop Culture.* Nashville: Thomas Nelson, 2015). P. XII.

The characters in *This Is Us* represent people just like you and me who struggle with all the same issues with which we struggle. By the end of this book, I trust you'll see that the people of the Bible are really us, too.

Not either/or but both/and

When my husband attended classes to get his Masters, he took a class called "Theology and Film." In it, the professor asked the students to watch a set of movies the professor had chosen for them. Some were R-rated and contained sexual and violent content. When asked to write a paper, my husband wrote about the disturbing content and said he was turned off by it. When asked to analyze the characters in the films, he spoke about the non-redemptive components of the characters.

The professor wrote a poignant comment on my husband's paper: "So, do you believe there are people that God cannot redeem?"

My husband said that really challenged him to rethink his position on how he viewed God and grace.

Grace does not escape anyone who seeks him wholeheartedly. To think so means there are some sins the blood of Christ does not cover. Christians would do well to analyze their positions on the people in our lives of whom we believe are not worthy of God's redemptive grace.

So often we forget the heart of God embedded in the Bible. The Bible is not a set of rules that, when followed, stop or begin certain behaviors. Rather, it's a love letter from a loving God to his children.

When I think about the love notes my children have given me, I smile at their innocence. The children presented the notes with such pride, often saying, "Mom, look what I made you!" Their hearts swelled as I mused over how beautiful their drawings were and how talented the young "artists" were. To the naked eye, the sketches were just a bunch of scribblings made by children who simply couldn't create better images because of a lack of motor skills. They wrote how their brain perceived their world at that time in their young lives.

As they got older however, and they developed their skills *and* brains, they were capable of turning those simple shapes into images that did resemble recognizable shapes and people.

My point is this: When we are baby Christians, our minds can only comprehend what we are being told. We approach life with an innocence and trust that the leaders in our lives have all of the spiritual facts we could ever need. We interpret the Bible with the same simplicity and innocence as my kids did when they made those drawings. However, as we mature as disciples, we begin to not only read the Bible but we also study it and interpret it for ourselves using the resources and tools we have at our fingertips. No longer do we rely on being spoon-fed, but we begin to interact with the world of a new understanding of the world around us as we embrace a biblical and Christian worldview.

When Jesus called his disciples, he didn't choose the people who were the most desperate. He picked people who had the most to lose. Example: John and Andrew had solidified their futures by taking over the family fishing business, but they risked it all by dropping their nets to follow Jesus.

Following Jesus takes risks. It might seem down-right odd to not watch the most popular TV programs because of overly violent and sexual content. *Orange is the New Black* and the *Walking Dead* are two shows which content is too over the top for my taste. However, all Christians need to evaluate their sensitivities and decide what they can watch and what they cannot. Not all TV and movies are acceptable for all viewers. Make sure you are knowledgeable on the content in newer TV shows and movies (especially those on Netflix because they do not follow the same FCC laws) and decide ahead of time whether it is something you can rationalize viewing.

Robert McGee, author of <u>The Search for Significance</u> says, "As Christians, our fulfillment in this life depends not on our skills to avoid life's problems, but on our ability to apply God's specific solution to life's problems. An accurate understanding of God's truth is the first step toward discovering our significance and worth." [3] It's not enough to merely read the Word and go through the motions of the faith. We should strive to engage with it, understand it, and be able to apply those biblical truths to help those drowning in the false teachings of the world in which we live.

"Blurred Lines," a song written and produced by Robin Thicke, T.I, and Pharrell Williams, shattered records in 2013. According to Nielsen Soundscan Data, it was the biggest selling single of 2013, [5]as well as the longest-running single on the Billboard Music charts in the R and B/ Hip Hop category, knocking Mary J. Blige's single off the top spot which she held for over seven years.[4] It also topped the charts in over twenty countries.

But fame has a price, a price that has cost Thicke his marriage and his reputation in the music community.

Soon after the song's success, Thicke's wife filed for divorce amidst rumors and photos of him grabbing a woman's backside at a nightclub and his controversial performance at the MTV Video Music Awards with Miley Cyrus. In addition, he battled a private battle of drugs and alcohol addiction. In an article from People.com, Thicke told a prosecutor, "Every day I woke up, I would take a Vicodin to start the day, and then I would fill up a water

---

[3] McGee, Robert S. *The Search for Significance.* (Houston: Rapha Publishing, 1990.) p.14.

[4] Ramirez, Rauly. "Robin Thicke's 'Blurred Lines' Breaks Record atop Hot R&B/Hip-Hop Songs." *Billboard.* http://bit.ly/2yeo8WJ

bottle with vodka and drink it before and during my interviews… I was high and drunk every time I did an interview last year, so there are some quotes I don't remember saying, but I do generally remember trying to sell the public on the fact that 'Blurred Lines' was my idea in some way."[5]

Soon after the song's success, Marvin Gaye's family slapped Thicke and Williams with a lawsuit for copyright infringement, citing it sounded too much like Gaye's single "Got to Give It Up." In March of 2015, Thicke and Williams were found libel and paid the Gaye family 7.3 million dollars and 25 million in damages. The "Rolling Stone" article also stated that both Thicke and Williams received a little over five million for the single, which allowed them to keep little profit from the single's success. Thicke built his identity around how the world saw him without any thought about how the people closest to him saw him. He gained fame in the world's eyes but lost his soul (and family) in the process.

It's the same with culture. We don't need to be afraid of interacting with the pop culture and trends that are here today and gone tomorrow because if we are anchored to Christ, we will never be swayed. The only way we are anchored is if we understand and know the Word for ourselves and don't accept carte blanche what someone else told us. We might shelter our eyes and ears inside a Christian bubble, listening to only Christian music and

---

[5] Corriston, Michelle. "Robin Thicke: 'I Told My Wife the Truth and That's Why She Left Me'." *People Magazine*. http://bit.ly/2P8D5Rq

20

reading only Christian books and engaging in Christian activities. We tell ourselves we are "in the world, but not of the world" and that we should stay away from anything secular. When we see issues that contradict our morals, we think the answer is to shut the TV off and pretend that if, we don't engage in it, then somehow that's taking a stand and that everyone else will follow.

Unfortunately, with so many Christians with differing views on today's issues and pervasive contradictions to the Bible, we think we're doing the world a favor. But instead of leading the world into righteousness, we allow the world to lead us, taking a back seat and keeping our collective voices shut. Social media feeds are silent when we should be speaking out on issues that are on God's heart. We believe the lie that certain sins are under the blood of Christ and others are not.

So, how do we do that?

The Bible is a letter that convicts, challenges, encourages and spurs us on. If we yield our hearts to it, our lives will soon follow. The Bible is filled with stories of God's people who, through an intimate encounter with God, changed the world. They did it through interacting with the poor, the lonely, the righteous, and the sinners.

It's our calling to do the same. We may never be able to interact with celebrities one-on-one, but the way we engage with culture is through discussion and understanding. First, however, we have to know where culture is headed and trust there is someone who has already gone before us and serves as a standard for us to follow.

Perhaps the place where we should start is equipping the next generation with the ability to study and interpret Scripture to test and see if what someone is saying is true. In this new age of "alternative facts" and "fake news," children more than ever are questioning authority. It's not necessarily wrong to question whether the leaders of our churches are giving us true information. Rather, we need to know what to do when we find out it's not true. Children need to feel empowered that they too can know God intimately, and in doing so, it means connecting with God intimately. This may include engaging in spiritual disciplines such as silence and solitude, fasting, Scripture memorization, prayer, studying God's word, and journaling. I believe if children can learn the tools necessary to engage, they will become anchored in the faith and not be so easily swayed by the world.

Ephesians 4:11-16 says, "So Christ himself gave the apostles, the prophets, the evangelists, the pastors and teachers, to equip his people for works of service, so that the body of Christ may be built up until we all reach unity in the faith and in the knowledge of the Son of God and become mature, attaining to the whole measure of the fullness of Christ. Then we will no longer be infants, tossed back and forth by the waves, and blown here and there by every wind of teaching and by the cunning and craftiness of people in their deceitful scheming. Instead, speaking the truth in love, we will grow to become in every respect the mature body of him who is the head, that is, Christ. From him the whole body, joined and held together by every supporting ligament, grows and builds itself up in love, as each part does its work."

I'm not saying we should subject our children to programs that blur our lines of sensitivity and redirect our moral compasses. We do, however, need to be aware of what the next generation believes and thinks and understand that even though the Bible doesn't specifically talk about these issues, it *does* talk about something that is at the core of everything: the heart - "From out of the heart the mouth speaks" (Matthew 12:34).

At the time of this writing, there is wildfire spreading about a graphic scene depicted in the Netflix series *13 Reasons Why*. In it, a teen commits suicide in graphic detail. But the show raises eyebrows for some mental health professionals, while others praise the show, saying it is saving countless lives. "Some mental health experts say the show could pose health risks for certain young people, such as those who have suicidal thoughts. Others suggest the show provides a valuable opportunity to discuss suicide risk with young people, as well as teaching them how to identify warning signs of depression or suicidal thoughts among their peers. Among American young people, those between ages 10 and 24, suicide is the third leading cause of death, according to the US Centers for Disease Control and Prevention."[6]

From what you fill your eyes and heart with to how you behave, everything matters when it comes to becoming close to the heart of God. Rich Nathan and Insoo Kim, authors of the book Both/And help Christians achieve a balance between being in the world and not being of the world: "All the apostles taught Both/And Christianity... Compassion towards the weak and holiness toward God: we are not permitted to choose one over the other. We're always tempted to say: 'which is more important? God says, 'I want both!' The temptation is to say, "I'm making such a great difference in this world by feeding hungry people, that God no longer cares about what I do sexually.' God wants hungry people fed and he wants your sex life cleaned up. It is wonderful that you've adopted a child through world vision, but God also cares about your gossip. With God it is always Both/ And."[7]

As Christians, we are obligated to help those seeking God to strike that same balance. However, if we let everyone's sin go and not challenge people to be holy, it cheapens the grace promised to us in Christ. Justice and grace go hand in hand. That's why Paul says, "What shall we say, then? Shall we go on sinning so that grace may increase? By no means! We are those who have died to

---

[6] Howard, Jacqueline. "Why Teen Mental Health Experts Are Focused on '13 Reasons Why'." Cable News Network. https://cnn.it/2RraF6Y

[7] Nathan, Rich and Insoo Kim. *Both/And*. (IVP: Illinois: 2013). p. 13.

sin; how can we live in it any longer? Or don't you know that all of us who were baptized into Christ Jesus were baptized into his death?" (Romans 6:1-2.) If anyone understood God's grace, it was the apostle Paul. Known for persecuting Christians, once he had an encounter with Jesus, he turned his zeal for justice to Christians, to protecting them because they were now his brothers and sisters in Christ.

I would never suggest that to engage with culture you must make a child sit down and watch traumatizing graphic material in the name of culture engagement. However, I am saying that instead of simply turning away from the newest TV or Internet craze, we need to have open discussions about why the viewpoint expressed in a TV show or movie is wrong and open up the living Word and find out what it has to say about it. Allow your kids to speak openly and share their feelings and thoughts about the subject.

The book Reel Spirituality speaks to this issue when it says, "Dialogue between theology and movies can take many forms: it can note the explicit theological themes of given films or dialogue with the motifs embedded both in movies and the Bible. It can bring film and biblical (or theological) text into conversation, or it can compare and contrast the Christ of the Gospels with the political use of a Christ figure to advance the meaning of a given movie.... But whatever the shape, the common denominator in such approaches is the attempt to bring film and theology into two-way conversation, letting both sides be equal partners in the dialogue." [5]

Instead of throwing the children out into the world at the age of eighteen without the skills necessary to navigate a difficult world or without a firm foundation, let's equip our children with the tools necessary to not only take a stand against an ever-changing shift in views but also let them engage in the world, knowing they have put on the full armor of God and rest in the peace of knowing He will protect them and go before them.

The interesting thing about the armor of God is that the armor protected soldiers from the front, not the back. This was assuming that during the war, they always were going into battle, not retreating from it. The warriors' fronts, when engaged, were always protected; their backsides, however, were not. If we teach children to run away, the enemy will attack them at their weakest point. However, if we equip them with armor made from the strongest protection, they will engage in the battle, knowing they have already won the war.

---

[5] Johnston, Robert K. *Reel Spirituality.* (Grand Rapids: Baker academic: 2006.). p. 68.

*My point is, what's wrong with being normal?
Olivia, you're always talking about being real.
Right? That kiss that we had yesterday, that was
real. Those feelings were real, and I know that
you know that. And it doesn't shock me that you
are scared, right? You are horrified, so you're
trying to sabotage it. I understand that, but what
might be worse than that is I'm not sure you've
ever experienced something real your entire life.
I'm starting to feel like you attaching to something
that's not a calculated act is too much for your
empty human shell to handle. I feel sorry for you.*

Kevin

Chapter Three
Beyond "The Manny":
Finding Significance

When I was young, one of my favorite games to play was "Jenga." I'd stack each block neatly row by row, making sure each row was more stable than the one below. As each block was pulled out and placed at the top, however, the foundation became shakier with each move. Soon, no matter which block I tapped on, each one's stability was in question. As predicted, the tower's bottom became so unsteady, the whole tower eventually came crashing down.

In comparison, since I've been on a journey with God for twenty years, I've learned that the foundation of my life must be stable enough to hold whatever weight would be placed on top. No matter what life throws at me, if my foundation is not stable and ready to hold the weight of problems and unpredictable circumstances, my life will soon come crashing down.

Each of the Pearson siblings in the TV program struggles with the instability of their foundations too. Before hiring Kate as an assistant, the potential boss asks: "Why do you want this position? Your boss spoke about you in such glowing terms; why did you leave?" "Because I fell in love with him, and it wasn't a healthy situation," Kate replied. In fact, we find Kate in all kinds of unhealthy situations. From dumping the neighbor's dog poop on top of junk food she just threw away to binge eating powdered donuts in the gas station parking lot, Kate's life revolves around weight.

In episode four, we find the Pearson clan going on their first summer outing at the community swimming pool. Kate, dressed in her brand-new Care Bears two- piece swimsuit, saunters over to her friends and asks them if they want to play with her. This is the first time we see Kate being rejected because of her weight.

Audiences can also relate to Kate's rejection another time as she opens a letter from her friends. The letter contains nine words that pierce Kate's heart and, ultimately, her self-esteem: "You embarrass us. We don't want to play with you anymore" were words written right next to a drawing of a pig.

As children, we've all been victims of our friends' insulting jabs at our physical appearance. But the TV events indicate that this carries incredible weight (pun intended) toward Kate's distorted body image. Kate's identity is deeply enmeshed in Kevin's life as well. She even tells him, "I don't know who I would be if I wasn't your sister." Her identity is rooted in how others perceive her physical appearance and in her love relationships with men, which might have to do with the conversation she had with her father that fateful day at the swimming pool.

After reading the harsh note from Kate's friends, Kate's mother encourages her to put on a shirt. Her father gives her his shirt and tells her, "It's a magic T-shirt. When you wear it, your enemies will only see you the way you want to be seen. Whether it's a warrior or a princess, whatever you want."

When Kate asks if it works, the father replies, you tell me. I was wearing this shirt the night I met your mom, and she thought I was the handsomest man in the world.

"You?" Kate asks.

"Yeah, me. It's magic."

Putting on the shirt, Kate says, "I'm going to go with princess."

Jack, the three kids' father, replies, "I want you to know, Daddy already sees you that way, with or without the shirt."

But magic T-shirts only worked when she was a child. Her life revolves around weight so much, she breaks up with her new boyfriend Toby because she doesn't want his distraction of derailing her from her goals. She stalks Toby's slim and beautiful ex-wife because her insecurity about being overweight distorts her ability to see herself as the Father sees her.

Jack's speech to Kate is indicative of how the Father sees us, too. Before the fall, Adam and Eve were beautiful and perfect. God loved them both equally and unconditionally. But when they ate the forbidden fruit, their

31

body shaming began. Soon they no longer saw themselves the way God saw them. Now they saw themselves (and their bodies) as less than perfect, even when God saw them as good enough. Jack's speech is a beautiful portrayal of the way God sees His children, too.

Galatians 3:29 says, "If you belong to Christ, then you are Abraham's seed, and heirs according to the promise." According to this verse, we are heirs of God, and if God is the king, then we are princes and princesses! But in a world where Kate doesn't know the freedom her heavenly Father wants to offer her, she continues to search for another man who'll treat her like a princess like her earthly father did. She falls for Toby, a friend from her weekly food addicts' group. Toby pulls out all the stops to help Kate, from landing her a singing gig at a nursing home where his aunt lives to, literally, rolling out the red carpet and taking pictures of her, making it clear he wants her to feel like the star she is, even if she doesn't believe she is one.

Randall is looking to establish his identity as well. When he first meets his biological father, William, Randall makes a point to tell him about all the fancy things he has from his lucrative job as a weather commodities trader (We still don't quite know what that means.) He emphatically announces to his dad, "I don't need anything from you." Yet, when his father invites him to come in, he jumps at the chance.

Throughout the show, we see in flashbacks Randall's attempts as a child to find his biological parents. From approaching a black couple in the grocery store and asking them if they can roll their tongue to telling his black friends that his dad might be a cook, a basketball player, or a mailman (all professions in which Randall has observed black people doing), he is desperate to find the missing piece of himself. But it's not enough. We know this by Randall's lifelong search and final success in locating his birth father. As he communicates with William, Randall's compassion for him grows and grows. He invites William to live with his family after William tells Randall he has stage-four stomach cancer and does not have long to live. We weep for Randall, knowing he not only has to grieve his biological death but also his adopted father's death (Jack's death is revealed in another episode). Behind all the nice cars and big fancy house, Randall just wants to belong.

Kevin wants to belong, too, but in a different way. As the oldest child, he's had to fight to get his parents' attention. At a scene in a swimming pool, Kevin calls out to his dad to look at him as he dunks his head underwater, only to realize he has gone out too far into the pool and almost drowns. He gasps for air and struggles to breathe but manages to pull himself out of the water, only to find his parents distracted by Kate's and Randall's predicaments, thus never seeing Kevin struggle in the water.

Scenarios like this only result in Kevin wanting to be known for more than just a pretty face. Although he has achieved monster-style fame, it's still not enough. Engaging in meaningless one-night stands with women and shutting off his feelings, he quickly realizes that everyone in the world only knows him as "The Manny" and nothing more. Disliking his self-made prison, he realizes that caring more about what everyone thinks rather than doing what was right may not have been the best idea after all.

In a scene where he phones Randall after a long time, Randall asks, "You're calling me because you care about what I think?"

Kevin says, "I care about what everyone thinks. You know that." In an impulsive move, he moves to New York to try to land a spot in a Broadway play. Although the director and playwright both tell him is acting is subpar, he lands the role anyway simply because his Manny status will help give the play the publicity and ticket sales they want.

Yet, he is left wanting, too. Two out of three siblings have more money than they could ever need, but it's all meaningless to them because they can't have what they want: meaningful relationships with others and intimacy with a loving father who'd always given them his undivided attention and who always would see them as the favorite sibling.

Although this may seem like a new storyline, it's nothing new. Although Kevin, Kate, and Randall explore this in modern day, King Solomon knows this story all too well.

Surrounded by a concubine of women and all the wealth and wisdom he could ever need, he realizes he has created a type of "prison" for himself, too, except he has the keys to set himself free. This is how he begins his writings:

> "Meaningless! Meaningless!" says the Teacher. "Utterly meaningless! Everything is meaningless." What do people gain from all their labors at which they toil under the sun? Generations come and generations go, but the earth remains forever."

He continues: "I said to myself, 'Look, I have increased in wisdom more than anyone who has ruled over Jerusalem before me; I have experienced much of wisdom and knowledge.' Then I applied myself to the understanding of wisdom, and also of madness and folly, but I learned that this, too, is a chasing after the wind" (Ecclesiastes 1:1-4; 13-14).

Author Lysa Teurkeurst in the book <u>Uninvited</u> says, "The peace of our souls does not rise and fall with unpredictable people or situations. Our feelings will shift, of course. People do affect us. But the peace of our souls is tethered to all that God is. And though we can't forget his specific plans, the fact that God will work everything together for good is a completely predictable promise." [1]

---

[1] Teurkeurst, Lysa. *Uninvited.* (Tennessee: Thomas Nelson, 2016.) p.62.

When we put our faith and trust in Christ. He holds our hands as we go through the trials of life. Instead of running to the quick fix like food, relationships, or possessions, our foundation is solid. There's no fear that it will teeter and fall under the weight of the instability of fleeting pursuits.

For me, this is a day-to-day trust, especially when I take a step of faith, and the path that I am on is unsteady. For Kate, Kevin, and Randall, it's a revolution in thinking, a renewing of their minds. Although their dad is not there to give them a pep talk, that doesn't mean they can't walk in the freedom of who God has made them to be. Jack has told Randall often, "I want you to stick out. I want you to be different in all sorts of ways."

This Is Us allows us to take a journey into the unknown, into the instability of life. This show dares us to plug our noses and go into the deep part of the pool. Even if we sink into the deep waters, there's One who will never let us drown.

You see, for days, I've been plagued by the question: How do I honor my father's legacy? Then I realized, I honor his legacy by taking what I learned from the way he lived his life and use it to shape the way I go on living mine. So here it is, Tyler. I quit.

Randall

Chapter Four
The Big Three and the
Power of Community

One of the appeals of *This Is Us* is it's not just a source of entertainment, but it speaks to what our souls deeply long for. We long for a strong family connection and a bond so strong that nothing can stop it. Jack, in his button-down shirt and tie, gets ready to say goodbye to his wife and children before going to work but not before Jack and the kids recite their daily mantra as they pound their fists into their chests:

> "First came me, and Mom said gee; then came me, and Mom said wee; and then came me, and Dad said that's three. One, two, three, Big Three!"

This Is Us isn't a show; it's a battle cry. It's a promise that families stick together no matter what and fight the battles of life together.

Community is also a huge theme of the show. As viewers, we first get a hint into this strong community in the first episode when Kevin is at a party where two girls are in his room, and they are dancing. The phone rings, Kevin picks up, and everything stops because his twin sister Kate needs him.

Kate acts in the same way, even in the midst of Toby's grand gesture of landing Kate a singing gig at his aunt's nursing home. All kids wish they had this type of bond with their parents as they grew up. All parents wish they had kids who doted on them like Kevin, Kate, and Randall do to their dad. All people wish they had a place to belong and a community to which they could belong.

Randall desperately wants to know he belongs. At the suggestion of their neighbor Yvette, a black woman Randall met at the swimming pool, Jack takes Randall to a local karate class. There his black instructor instills in him that they're all a part of a community. The instructor asks Jack to lie down in a position to do a push-up then has Randall lie on Jack's back. As Jack does push-up after push-up, the instructor tells him, "As Randall's father you are his foundation. Your back was built to carry your son through life. Are you willing to hold him up, no matter what comes his way?"

"Yes," Jack says.

As Jack continues to do push-ups, the instructor continues: "Are you willing to raise this boy into a strong man? Are you willing to push him to be the best man he can be? Are you willing to lift him to greater heights even when it hurts?"

Although the instructor tells Jack to stop, Jack keeps going, push-up after exhausting push-up to prove to Randall that Jack wants and can be all the father he ever needs.

Similarly, when Kate finds out her mom is selling the cabin where they all spent their summers together as a family, Kate wants her, Kevin, and Randall to visit there one last time. Upon entering the cabin, they come across a painting where many dots on the artwork look like a mess, but when the eyes relax, the dots meld together into a single picture. As Randall imagines talking with his deceased father, his father reminds him, "It's all right here. You just have to relax your eyes and look right through it. It's right there in front of you."

It's tough to relax your eyes when it looks like you are alone. Throughout the episode, Kevin never sees the real picture behind the dots, much like his life. The things that are most important are right in front of him; yet, he struggles to find community through a litany of sleeping around and temporary jobs that make him lots of money but never satisfy his soul. Feeling like her world is unraveling after just breaking up with Toby, Kate goes into the woods alone, but Kevin follows her.

"I can't do this without my brothers," Kate says through tears.

"I need you here, Kate, I need you real bad," Kevin replies.

Neither Kevin nor Kate can figure out who they are apart from each other. Although this attitude may on some levels be unhealthy, it's also a demonstration of the unshakable bond family can be for each other.

41

Perhaps the most revealing component of the episode is Randall's revelation of how alone his mother was all her life. Keeping the secret that she knew the identity of Randall's biological father ostracized her from the community, which the family had already established. Randall tells Rebecca, "Keeping that secret for all those years must have been very lonely for you." Now that Kate, Kevin, and Randall are old enough to face life's trials, they only have themselves to rely on. It *is* difficult to battle life alone.

Jesus knew that. His disciples also knew that. In the face of persecution and loneliness for their beliefs, they had to rely upon themselves. When Jesus trained his disciples and sent them out to do the work of healing the sick and driving out demons, he sent them out two by two:

> "When Jesus had called the Twelve together, he gave them power and authority to drive out all demons and to cure diseases, and he sent them out to proclaim the kingdom of God and to heal the sick. He told them: "Take nothing for the journey— no staff, no bag, no bread, no money, no extra shirt. Whatever house you enter, stay there until you leave that town. If people do not welcome you, leave their town and shake the dust off your feet as a testimony against them." So they set out and went from village to village, proclaiming the good news and healing people everywhere" (John 9:1-6).

It sounds cruel, but Jesus understood that sending them out like lambs among wolves would take more than one person to accomplish His work. They would need each other to encourage and build each other up along the journey when things got rough. They would need to rely on each other's strength to lift them up when they didn't have enough strength to make it on their own.

The disciples had that in each other. Despite how difficult their circumstances were, despite the fact they gave up everything familiar for a leap into the unknown with Jesus, they had that bond in common. They weren't just strangers or mere acquaintances; they were family.

They didn't have a catchy phrase to repeat to themselves; instead, they had the living God right in front of them, walking along with them side-by-side. The disciples understood the power of relying on each other, especially after Jesus was resurrected:

> "They devoted themselves to the apostles' teaching and to fellowship, to the breaking of bread and to prayer. Everyone was filled with awe at the many wonders and signs performed by the apostles. All the believers were together and had everything in common. They sold property and possessions to give to anyone who had need. Every day they continued to meet together in the temple courts. They broke bread in their homes and ate together with glad and sincere hearts, praising God and enjoying the favor of all the people. And the Lord

added to their number daily those who were being saved" (Acts 2:42-47).

When I was twenty years old, my parents threw me out of my home because of my conversion from Catholicism to become a born-again Christian. That event remains one of the most soul-shaping experiences of my life. It taught me not only to trust God in a "clutching onto him for dear life" sort of way but also taught me about the power of the body of Christ. My Christian brothers and sisters in Christ provided for me in ways beyond what I could have ever hoped or dreamed. They became my family. I leaned on them when I had no strength and they encouraged me when I needed encouragement. They pushed me to be brave and to trust God even when I didn't see or think he was there.

As scary as that season in my life was, I realize now it's God's desire for all his children to rely on each other and not pursue the temporary fixes of the world that divide us rather than unite us. When we hold onto to each other and trust God in the midst of trouble, he surprises us in unexpected ways.

When I chose God over my family's expectations, he placed into my life a wonderful man who was soon to become my husband. I also now understand my calling and purpose, which he's allowing me the opportunity to live out. It may not have come in the way or timing that I would have chosen, but I wouldn't trade my decision for anything in the world.

The bond of family is what keeps Kate, Kevin, and Randall going. When things get rough, Kevin and Kate lean on the bonds of being twins to get through. Each one gives each other pep talks.

This is evident in the first episode when Kate hurts her ankle stepping on the scale. She says to Kevin, "I had this whole dream life planned out for myself. [I would have] A real career. I would marry a man like Dad, I would be a mom like Mom. But look at me Kev. I ate my dream life away."

Kevin says, "What is it you want me to say? Tell me what the magic phrase is."   "Tell me to quit feeling sorry for myself, tell me to wake up, tell me to lose the weight."

Kevin replies, "Quit feeling sorry for yourself, and that can start right now. Wake up! And what was the third thing?"

"Lose the weight," he says.

"What was that again?" Kevin asks.

"I'm going to lose the weight."

They already have the courage and the confidence to do the hard things necessary to accomplish their goals, but they just need that nudge from their family that they're doing the right thing.

That's what we Christians need, too. Instead of focusing on what we are up against in life, sometimes we need to just give each other a little nudge, to be there for each other, and give the pep talk when someone needs it, or just let each other know we're going in the right direction. As Christians we all have a place within the body of Christ.

Second Corinthians 12:12-19 speaks to this issue:

"Just as a body, though one, has many parts, but all its many parts form one body, so it is with Christ. For we were all baptized by one Spirit so as to form one body—whether Jews or Gentiles, slave or free—and we were all given the one Spirit to drink. Even so the body is not made up of one part but of many. Now if the foot should say, "Because I am not a hand, I do not belong to the body," it would not for that reason stop being part of the body. And if the ear should say, "Because I am not an eye, I do not belong to the body," it would not for that reason stop being part of the body. If the whole body were an eye, where would the sense of hearing be? If the whole body were an ear, where would the sense of smell be? But in fact God has placed the parts in the body, every one of them, just as he wanted them to be. If they were all one part, where would the body be? As it is, there are many parts, but one body."

Kevin, of all the characters, seems to understand the importance of community the best when he shows his nieces a picture of a painting he made. On the surface, it looks like a jumbled mess of colors. But he goes on to say that each color has a place in the painting, and that without each color there would be no paintings at all:

"Life is full of color, we each get to come along and add our own color to the painting. Even though it is not very big, the painting you have to figure goes on and on in each direction, like to infinity, because that is kind of like life, right? It's kind of crazy if you think about it. One hundred years ago some guy that I never met came to this country with a suitcase. He had a son, who had a son, who had me. So at first, I was thinking you know, maybe up here was that guy's part of the painting, and maybe over here was that guy's part of the painting. Then I started to think maybe we're all in the painting everywhere. I mean, before we were born, and after we die, and these colors that we keep adding, maybe they just keep adding one on top of another until eventually we're not even different colors anymore, we're just one thing. One painting. My dad's not with us anymore; he's not alive, but he's with us. He's with me every day. It all just fits somehow, even if we don't understand it yet. People will die, people we love, maybe tomorrow, maybe in the future. It's all kind of beautiful if you think about it. Just because someone dies, just because you can't see him anymore, doesn't mean they they're not still in the painting. I think that is the point of the whole thing. There's no dying, no you, no me, no them. It's just us, and this sloppy, wild, magical thing that has no beginning and no end is right here. I think it's us."

Our souls are crying out. We are desperate to know and be known and to belong to one body. We want to know that our brothers and sisters have our backs. God longs for us to unite, pump our fists in the air in solidarity, and let our war cries bellow from deep within. The cry of the father's heart is for all of his children to be a part of the Big Three—Father, Son and Holy Spirit.

Then you make it. You deserve it. You deserve the beautiful life you made. You deserve everything, Randall. My beautiful boy. My son. I haven't had a happy life. Bad breaks. Bad choices. A life of almosts and could haves. Some would call it sad, but I don't 'cause the two best things in my life were the person in the very beginning and the person at the very end, and that's a pretty good thing to be able to say, I think.

William

Chapter Five
Making Lemonade Out of Lemons

Jack and Rebecca Pearson are dealt the sourest of lemons in episode one of *This is Us*. Going into early delivery, Rebecca and Jack have a high-risk pregnancy; she's pregnant with triplets. They're thrown a sudden curveball when Dr. Kavotsky must step in for their regular doctor, Dr. Snyder, whose appendix burst and can't be with her to guide her though the delivery. From the first moments of the story of Rebecca and Jack, we understand that they have to put their trust and hope in someone whom they've never met or seen before. However, he assures them he's more than capable of getting the job done.

We Christians can relate, can't we? Isn't that the story behind our story? Regardless of whatever life throws our way, we are asked to trust and hope in the One whom we have never seen or known before. Yet, our trust in Him is more than capable of guiding us through the journey.

Dr. Kavotsky (or Dr. K., as he is lovingly called) guides them not only through the delivery but eventually through life as well. In the pilot episode, he says to Jack and Rebecca after his introduction, "I'm 73 years old. You know what that means, don't you? It means I can't run wind sprints as fast as I used to, but my faculties are, otherwise, completely intact. There are days I wish they weren't because then I could retire and spend my remaining days doing something more glamorous than pulling eight-pound objects out of women's vaginas. But until that time, I keep showing up here every day, all right? I'm also aware that I'm a complete stranger to you, and that this is the biggest moment of your life. Honey, listen to me, I'm the best of the best, and I swear to you on the lives of my children and on my grandchildren that I am up to the task, all right? Now, which one of you is pregnant?"

In an emotional monologue, Dr. K. gives Jack an intimate glimpse into his life after delivering the news to Jack that his third child has died. "I lost my wife last year to cancer. It's the reason why I still work so much at my age. Just trying to pass the time. We were married fifty-three years. Five children; eleven grandkids. The reason I went into this field, truth be told. I have spent five decades delivering babies, more babies than I can count. But not a single day goes by that I don't think about the baby I lost. I'd like to think that, because of the child I lost, because of the path he sent me on, I have saved countless other babies. I'd like to think that when you are an old man like me you took the sourest lemon that life had to offer and turned it into something resembling lemonade. If you can do that, then you'll still be taking three babies home from the hospital. I might be senile, but I thought it ought to be said."

It's not easy to make lemonade out of lemons, is it? In fact, it's nearly impossible. When you're drowning in tears because the child you said goodbye to yesterday is no longer here, or you walk into work to see your desk cleared off, it's easy to want to dwell on the negative. When you

52

feel like life is constantly pushing you down and you cry out to God for help, but all you hear is silence, it's downright impossible to find joy.

But joy is not an emotion.

Carol Mcleod, a speaker and author, believes joy is the atmosphere that surrounds the throne of God. "When I am being overtaken by the deceit of my emotions, what I really need is more of Him. In order to cultivate the joy of Heaven's grandeur in my puny, ordinary life, I need more of his presence and more time spent at his beautiful nail-scarred feet."[1]

She eloquently communicates that the joy "is found wherever He is. He is in every sunset. His presence is visible in the first flowers of spring and in the glorious leaves of fall. His voice is heard in the symphony of worship and in the giggle of a baby. His presence resounds in the roar of the ocean waves and in the majesty of snow-capped mountains. He is found gently caressing his own in the trauma of emergency rooms and in the aftermath of violent storms. He is found comforting widows and brokenhearted parents. He is there in the humdrum of daily life when the dishes are piled high, the laundry is mountainous and the bills never end. He is there in the unending days of loneliness and in the piles of tissues by

---

[1] Burton McLeod, Carol. *Joy for All Seasons*. (Florida: Bridge Logos, 2016.) p. 2.

your bed. He is with you, and you with Him, and He brings the gift of Heaven's joy! " [2]

Joy is not something to be merely felt but lived. Joy is found in the way we react to both positive and negative circumstances in life. That's why James says, "Consider it pure joy, my brothers and sisters, whenever you face trials of many kinds, because you know that the testing of your faith produces perseverance. Let perseverance finish its work so that you may be mature and complete, not lacking anything" (James 1:1-4).

It's interesting that the way I choose to react to my circumstances sets in motion the ability to create deep transformation within my soul. So, could it be that demonstrating *outward* reactions such as gratitude and joy (even when I don't feel like it) produces the *inner* transformation needed to make me more like Jesus?

If anyone has an excuse to wallow in their circumstances, it's Jack and Rebecca. A young couple, looking at the world wide-eyed with so many possibilities, plan on being parents to triplets. Expecting to go home with three babies, they are dealt a horrific blow. The death of a child is one of the worst things that can ever happen to a couple. It would be easy for them to get angry at God and angry at each other, looking inward at what they lost instead of looking at the other possibilities that lie before them. What a wonderful opportunity that happened, seemingly by circumstances beyond their control. They see

---

[2] Ibid.

their circumstances as bittersweet. They grieve their loss but then take the opportunity that lies before them.

What's interesting is also to see life from the fireman's perspective. Dealing with a marriage on the brink of divorce, Fireman Joe finds a divine opportunity, too. Seeing baby Randall on the doorstep of the firehouse, he sees it as an opportunity to fix his failing marriage. Since Joe and his wife couldn't have kids, this was the opportunity they had been waiting for: a quick fix to solve their difficulties. But his wife understands it will only complicate matters because her issues and Joe's issues as well go way deeper than just having a baby.

Turning divine appointments into opportunities takes risk. If the fireman and his wife had jumped into that opportunity, Randall's life could have been much different. Perhaps he would have become a fireman rather than the weather commodities trader he did become. He might not have gone to the private school that sent him on the trajectory toward his future career goals. Maybe he wouldn't have been full of anxiety, desperately trying to perform to receive everyone's approval.

Joy can be found in divine appointments.

Randall's appearance on the same day that Rebecca delivered six weeks early was no accident. It was a divine appointment. And if Dr. K. hadn't been available, they wouldn't have had the mentor they had throughout their lives raising their kids. Similarly, Dr. K. wouldn't have been influenced by Jack and Rebecca's leap of faith in adopting Randall and moving on with their life after tragedy.

By the end of the first episode of *This is Us*, we're already challenged to be different both as Christians and as people. Jack and Rebecca dare us to be bold to laugh at the trials in our lives and embrace the divine opportunities God places in our lives as instruments of transformation not circumstances in which to wallow because they were not what we had in mind.

Divine opportunities happen all the time. We just have to open our eyes and be aware. The car that broke down in the middle of the driveway spared you from a possible accident on the highway. That job you suddenly loss was causing you to miss church and other opportunities to fellowship with other believers. Losing your job frees you to serve within your local church body and find another job whose co-workers need your demonstrations of God's grace and testimonies of God's goodness. Instead of lamenting at the losses, revel in the gains. Cling onto the train of Jesus' robe. Jesus was faithful in healing the woman with a physical ailment because of her boldness to cling onto him.

God will be faithful in doing the extraordinary within your ordinary day. You just have to be open to His providence in your life.

Joy and Intentionality

Recently, we had some severe weather rip through our area. Although it's not a natural occurrence, we had a tornado warning, causing my family and me to take shelter at our church next door in the basement. As the lights flickered and the wind howled, we all prayed we would make it through. With God's mercy and provision we did make it through with minimal damage. An hour later, the once green-colored storm clouds blew over, giving way to a gorgeous sunset. Then a rainbow appeared among the clouds.

In the Old Testament, a rainbow appeared after the flood as a promise that flooding of that magnitude would ever occur again. When we saw that rainbow, it reminded me of a revelation: It's a natural part of the process for a rainbow to appear. In science, a rainbow appears when rain droplets intersect with the sunshine, causing the rain to reflect beautiful, splendid color. In fact, it would be unnatural and a contradiction to the natural order of things for a rainbow not to appear. My point is this: Even amidst the storm, a rainbow always appears. You just have to look for it.

Embracing joy takes intentionality. It means putting one foot in front of the other. It means facing reality in trust every day, focusing on God's will and not your own. Maturity in Christ means trusting that God knows what's best and willing to surrender your will for God's will.

As someone who tends to look at the negative circumstances in life rather than the positive, counting life's trials as joy is not a natural process for me. I have to practice it, so it becomes second nature to me.

In a later episode, we get a glimpse into Dr. K.'s life before and after meeting Jack and his family. As Dr. K. mentioned, he had lost his wife to cancer after fifty-three years of marriage and works to pass the time. After us understanding what his life is like, we then understand it's just a bit more than just a simple way to pass the time.

Dr. K. is stuck. He spends his morning eating the same cereal and talking to his wife as if she is sitting next to him at the dining room table. His kids, although well intentioned to talk to their father and get him to enjoy life a bit more, make him feel like their mother was a burden on them.

After meeting Jack and Rebecca, his life changes. He begins to get rid of his wife's things. He begins to let go of his wife. He has dinner with a neighbor who has taken an interest in him. Dr. K. demonstrates that despite great sorrow, beauty can come out of that sorrow. Simply because he moves on with his life doesn't mean he doesn't still love his wife. Joy doesn't come by wallowing in the past; it comes when we trust the One who holds our past, present, and future.

Joy in the Midst of Trials

If I'm honest, I'm struggling to write this chapter. Life for me hasn't been filled with roses and sunshine. Since the day I gave my life to Christ, my life has been filled with highs and lows, ups and downs. There are moments when I could barely breathe, unsure if I was going to make it through until the next day. Then there have been other days when I have been convinced I have experienced a taste of the fullness of joy I will receive in heaven.

After over seventeen years in pastoral ministry, I have watched parents dedicate their babies in lifelong service and submission to God. I have been at the bedsides of those who are taking their last breaths, and I've been in the audience to watch two people make a lifelong commitment to each other in holy matrimony. It has been a privilege. But I have also sat bewildered when people whom I considered good friends stabbed my husband and me in the back, the sting of which lasted months, severely impairing my impartial judgment of the church body.

Maybe the reason why I'm struggling with the concept of joy is because I'm not sure I have ever experienced joy. I have had joyful *emotions,* but I'm not sure I understand what joy is in relation to difficult circumstances and how to exude that joy when the bottom has fallen out of my world and I feel like I'm free falling into oblivion if I listen to my heart or rationalize joy in my head. So, I go to the Scriptures because I know that if I do, God will guide and direct my path.

Here's what I've discovered about joy:

- "I rejoice in following your statutes as one rejoices in great riches" (Psalm 119: 14).

- "Until now you have not asked for anything in my name. Ask and you will receive, and your joy will be complete" (John 16:24).

- "Be joyful in hope, patient in affliction, faithful in prayer" (Romans 12:12).

- "Therefore if you have any encouragement from being united with Christ, if any comfort from his love, if any common sharing in the Spirit, if any tenderness and compassion, [2] then make my joy complete by being like-minded, having the same love, being one in spirit and of one mind" (Philippians 2:1-3).

- "Though you have not seen him, you love him; and even though you do not see him now, you believe in him and are filled with an inexpressible and glorious joy, for you are receiving the end result of your faith, the salvation of your souls" (1 Peter 1:8-9).

Given these verses, this is what I have concluded:

- Abiding in God results in joy.

- Joy is not an emotion that fluctuates with my circumstances. Rather, it is a result of obedience to God's calling, resulting in my salvation.

- My joy is complete when I'm one in spirit with others and selflessly give to others.

Pastor Ben Reaoch, author of the article "One Joy Above Others," puts it beautifully when he says:

> "Our souls are hungry. We have deep emotional and spiritual and relational cravings that we're often not even fully aware of. But instead of looking to the Bread of Life, we are so easily enticed by food that perishes.
>
> We may often (even subconsciously) try to satisfy our deep heart hungers by overindulging other appetites. We try to satisfy ourselves with excessive food or drink. We seek immoral pleasure in another person or on a screen. We pamper ourselves with unnecessary comforts, like never-ending Netflix or mind-dulling social media and games.
>
> In John 6, Jesus feeds the five thousand and then proclaims, 'I am the bread of life' (John 6:35.) Jesus also says to the crowd, 'Do not work for the food that perishes, but for the food that endures to eternal life, which the Son of Man will give to you' (John 6:27).

As we begin to see the dysfunction and misguided desires within ourselves, we learn more clearly how satisfying Jesus really is. Consider these four self-diagnostic questions to discern your heart hungers, and whether you're seeking the Bread of Life or merely food that perishes."[3]

Joy is the fulfillment our souls crave. It satisfies when the temporal things of the world don't. Joy is the choice to trust God even when we don't see, feel, or hear him. Joy is choosing to see a light in the midst of darkness. In fact, it's the light we use to illuminate our lives when the enemy tries to snuff it out.

The Ripple Effect of Joy

One year on our annual vacation to Maine, we rented a small cottage that overlooks a gorgeous pond. I often would sit for hours in silence inhaling the fresh, crisp air and enjoying the majestic view. One day, I sat in my oversized, brown lounge chair and watched in delight as my son threw rocks into the pond. I marveled at how one small rock could cause such a disturbance to the otherwise placid water. As soon as the rock hit the water, it made such a splash that it not only made one ripple, but it made three others after it. I found it amazing that one small piece of God's creation could have such a large impact on the world around it.

---

[3] Reaoch, Ben., "One Joy Lasts Forever." Desiring God. http://bit.ly/2Qw8FJo

This is true of any relationship. We have the opportunity to produce an effect on everyone's life. Just like that rock, we change lives merely by our presence. We impact lives positively and negatively. As Christians, we choose to impact lives through our calling to make disciples.

Although many people believed the episode featuring Dr. K. was an unnecessary episode, I think it's a brilliantly placed one. I loved seeing how our actions negatively and positively affect others, even when we don't see it. When we embrace joy in our lives, that joy spreads. Others embrace joy because our joy attracts them to us. Like a magnet, people are drawn to those that seem to embrace life's trials with trust and hope rather than with despair and negativity.

Although Jack and Rebecca would have chosen differently, they got Dr. K. after their regular doctor had a medical emergency. What they didn't know was that Dr. K. was exactly what they needed because he wasn't just a doctor. He became their mentor, knowing they needed someone to help them guide them through life's difficulties.

In the episode titled "Christmas Eve," Jack and Rebecca are summoned when Dr. K. goes in for surgery for a medical issue of his own. Due to the fact they were alerted when Dr. K. went into surgery, we realize Dr. K. has been a part of their lives for many years, well after the birth of their babies.

It'll be interesting to see how their relationship unfolds as the seasons go on, but for now, that one chance encounter changed their whole lives, as well as Dr. K.'s. As previously stated, from the difficulty of letting go of his wife, Dr. K. is stuck. His speech regarding making something resembling lemonade out of the sourest lemons and what life has to offer, we see Dr. K. doesn't practice what he preaches. But little does he know, he needed Jack and Rebecca as much as Jack and Rebecca needed him.

Writer Megan Vick comments:

"The episode visited Dr. K. on the morning of the Big Three's birth to show him still in the thralls of depression after losing his wife a little more than a year before. Her clothes still hang in their closet. He still talks to her at the breakfast table and informs her of what he's preparing to do that day. Even though Dr. K's eldest son implores him to try and move on with his life, it's clear that the doctor isn't ready to leave the memory of his wife behind. In another tear-jerking scene, Dr. K goes to visit his wife's grave and confesses that he doesn't know how to live without her. There's more than a subtle hint that the older man is ready join his wife in the afterlife, but before he can complete the thought, he gets a page that he's needed at the hospital. It's the call to deliver the Pearson triplets. Now, fans can see that Dr. K's dry humor was a facade to hide the pain he was feeling earlier in the day, but they can also see how Jack's determination and optimism

64

help to bring Dr. K from the brink as well. Of course, Jack and Rebecca lose their third child in delivery. The genius of Tuesday's episode was to show that Dr. K's heartfelt speech to Jack in the hospital hallway not only gave the Pearson patriarch the strength he needed to keep his family from falling apart, but also showed how Jack's pure love for his family was also enough to save Dr. K." [3]

Just like the rocks that made the ripple in the water. Our joy is far reaching, making an impact far beyond what we can even imagine. We just have to make a daily choice to pursue it and pursue it wholeheartedly.

---

[3] Vick, Megan. "This Is Us: Gerald McRaney on His Heartbreaking Return as Dr. K." TV Guide Today's News. http://bit.ly/2Qrohh9

When a white family adopts a black child and doesn't introduce themselves to any of us, we tend to take notice.

Yvette to Rebecca

Chapter Six
Swimming Pools, Maternity Wards and Mentorship

One of the first episodes in which we get an intimate look into the Pearsons' lives is when Jack wants to take the kids to the community pool to take a break from the summer heat. Packing all the kids up in the car, they finally get to the pool. The first thing they do is fight to claim a set of chairs together so they can sit by the pool. An already crowded area, the chairs are hard to come by. Throughout the episode, we see them fighting to make sure no one steals the chairs (Can you relate?) While Jack and Rebecca battle for chairs, they also battle to keep an eye on all three kids as Jack and Rebecca keep them from harm as they play. Kate finds a group of girls she wants to hang around with. Randall finds a random black family to play with, and Kevin vies for his dad's attention. Although this seems like an ordinary episode, it also gives us an insightful glimpse into how the consequences they suffer as kids follow them into their adult life. This is the episode in which Kate gets a letter from her friends. If the TV audience doesn't love this family already, they do in this episode.

With the large noise of the crowds at the pool, Kevin struggles to get his dad's attention, only to discover that his parents had never seen him almost drown. They're too busy looking for Randall, who has found a black family at the opposite end of the pool to play with. Randall has a pad of paper that he writes down the names of every black person he finds, so he can find his birth parents. When

Rebecca finds him, she brings him back to their area as the mother named Yvette tells her, "You should give him a proper haircut." She then explains that black hair is different and needs to be cared for accordingly. Humiliated, Rebecca takes him without responding. After pondering the woman's words, Rebecca swallows her pride and approaches Yvette again, asking her questions about how to care for his hair and whether or not he needs sunscreen. It's apparent in that episode that Randall keeps his relationship with the woman because she is found in a picture on the mantle of his adult home.

Remember…Kate is embarrassed by her weight. Kevin struggles to be seen and get the attention he has always wanted. Randall struggles with his identity and who he is. These are all issues the big three carry with them into their adult lives. It's later on in the season that the person they had leaned on for advice and support, their father Jack, has passed away, leaving them to rely solely on each other to get through the trials of their lives.

Rebecca fully understood that rearing Randall on her own was too daunting of a task. She knew she had to enlist the help of someone who not only knew how to help her but also someone who had lived through it herself. As a black woman, that person could offer much more insight to Rebecca than anyone else. She could help her make choices on whether to send Randall to a private, yet predominantly white, school. She could help her with his increasing anxiety issues. Rebecca needed a mentor, someone to take her under her wing and teach her how to handle each situation as it came along.

But not all mentoring relationships are created equal.

In an article titled, "Mentoring Tips: Four Key Questions to Ask Before You Begin the Relationship," author Sherry Surratt says, "While mentoring can be lots of work and can certainly go wrong, I'm not giving up. God designed us to need community and to learn from each other. With the right questions up front, the relationship can be incredibly rich and rewarding for both sides." [1] She also suggests figuring out what type of relationship you want with your mentor. Will it be one in which both parties benefit each other through knowledge, expertise and prayer, or will it be one in which the more experienced person acts as a teacher to the other, doling out information and advice and the other passively receives it? When mentoring, Surratt suggests figuring out what you want to get out of the relationship as well as what each meeting will look like (i.e. will you read through a book together, and will both parties put in an equal amount of work?) It also will be beneficial to know the expectations of the mentor: Is that person strictly a friend, or will both be sharing their life experiences with each other?

---

[1] Surratt, Sherry. "Mentoring Tips." Today's Christian Woman. http://bit.ly/2QsO3By

Mentoring is the Gateway to Connection

According to an article in "Lifeway Magazine," mentoring still holds the key to connecting the generations in real and tangible ways: "Far from a 'leave us alone' mentality, today's young adults are very interested in learning from, interacting with, and forming bonds with previous generations. This desire for connection with people outside of their age demographic can be seen as a subset of the overall desire for relationships and community, but because of the specific and unique nature of these particular relationships, the characteristic of 'connection' stands on its own. According to their research:

- 45 percent of unchurched young adults identified the opportunity to receive advice from people with similar life experiences as very important.

- 68 percent of churched young adults identified the opportunity to receive advice from people with similar life experiences as very important."[2]

We all need people to mentor us, someone who is willing to encourage and disciple us so we can grow in our relationships with Christ. As much as I want to have close friendships, however, being a pastor's wife puts up this invisible barrier between the people within my church and me. It's a wall no one acknowledges but still exists nonetheless. It's a wall that prevents us from experiencing

---

[2] LifeWayStaff. "Biblical Model of Mentoring."
http://lfwy.co/2ydwRIY

the same intimate friendships that other members get to enjoy. That wall prevents me from venting to another congregation member when issues and tensions arrive amongst its leadership. It's a wall I try hard to chisel away to see inside people's hearts. But no matter how hard I try, I only get a glimpse inside. The wall still covers up the majority of their hearts as well as mine.

I knew I needed mentorship. But how do I as a pastor's wife achieve the intimate friendships I crave? I prayed and asked God to bring to mind someone who could fill that role but also could be someone outside the church fellowship so I could have someone to talk to if I was struggling. The Lord in his faithfulness laid someone on my heart. I mustered up the courage and asked her an important question: "Will you mentor me?"

I knew I was placing myself in a vulnerable position, but I knew she was what I needed. Within a few months of weekly phone calls, we had forged an unlikely friendship. Although we are both writers, we are in different stages of life. She, a woman in her seventies, strives to gain exposure for the ministry she shares with two other women as they minister to churches throughout the state. Yet, she blesses me in so many other ways. She is the Jonathan to my David, and she is someone with whom I trust to push me to the next level in my spiritual growth. In any other circumstance, I might not have gravitated to her because of our different circumstances and the wide age gap between us. However, she teaches me about things I can't learn in a Bible study or manufacture on a Sunday morning. She teaches me about the importance of accountability, slowing down and enjoying the small pleasures in life, being content no matter what the future holds, and living every day to the fullest.

When we connect only with those who walk, talk, and look like us, we taste the sweet fare of the fellowship Jesus longs for us to have. But when we step out of our comfort zones and make friends with someone who is different from us, our lives are enriched. This affords the opportunity to savor the deep, intimate connections given to us when someone shows us how to look at life from a different perspective. And I wouldn't have it any other way.

Instead of the finger wagging of older generations, church members desire people who are willing to share their experiences as an "I'm just like you" relationship not an "I know better than you" relationship. That's what Rebecca wanted. She wanted someone to come alongside of her, give her a compassionate hug, and help her along in her rearing of Randall. Instead, she got a finger wag and public shaming. She got "the boy needs a proper haircut" with a snub and a look as though Yvette was better than her. Yvette's response to Rebecca's apology that Randall had snuck over to sit next to her family was "Yes, I know who you are. When someone doesn't introduce herself to us with that boy, we find out who you are." It was an awkward encounter at best and a cruel conversation at worst. Rebecca, already feeling insecure about her ability to parent, didn't need that woman criticizing her every move, did she?

Apparently, Rebecca needed Yvette more than she thought. That woman became a staple to Rebecca's circle of friends, Randall often going over there to play on a regular basis as a child. Apparently, mentors have a way of impacting our lives more than we realize.

At first it didn't seem like Yvette was going to be a mentor. She didn't seem like she had any respect for Rebecca. Yet, she realized they needed to stick together. As a mom, she probably knew a bit about rejection. She knew what it was like to get dirty looks and stares from people simply for being out in public. She knew what it was like not to have people like her simply because of what she looked like. It was a commonality she shared with both Rebecca and Randall. It's not until she smiles at Rebecca that we understand who she really is—a mother who had been through it too and now was willing to share what little knowledge she had with Rebecca.

We all wish we had someone like that in our lives.

Mentoring as the Meta-Narrative of Our Lives

In an article from the Washington post titled "Why We're Obsessed with the Hit Show *This is Us*," author Russell Moore says:

"At the same time, though, we see them as children, and we see there's not all that much distance between the two. We see a glimpse of the way the decisions made in private of a young couple who never planned to be parents reverberate through the years in the lives of their offspring. This rings true because we all tend to see our lives as narrative and, like the characters in this series, the narrative is often murkier than we would like. Some of us had relatively idyllic childhoods. Some of us grew up in the specter of violence or addiction or abuse or some other awful reality. Some of us grew up wondering, as we do as we see some of the secrets of the back stories of this series unfold, whether the family figures of our past are heroes or villains or a mixture of the two. The switching back and forth between the 1980s and 2016 reminds us that the narrative of our lives is not a straight line. Our childhoods aren't just "back there," but they intrude on our lives now, sometimes in picking at old scars and sometimes in reminding us of the small mercies that have brought us safe thus far. We wouldn't be who we are if not for the stories that have made us — stories we love, stories we hate, and sometimes stories we long to peer into but leave us in mystery."[3]

This is how we should feel about the mentoring process, too. Whether *This is Us* lasts for three seasons or

[3] Moore, Russell Moore. "Why We're Obsessed with the Hit Show This Is Us." *The Washington Post.* https://wapo.st/2xYMKUa

twenty, one thing is clear: The Pearson family will go down in TV history as one of the most beloved families in history. They will be as well-known as the Cosbys, the Keatons, and the Bravermans. NBC has found a home for yet another ordinary (yet relatable) family, a family who takes us on a journey battling life's most difficult issues and lets us know we are not alone. Mentoring is like that, too. We all need someone to walk with and to hold our hands then tell us everything is going to be okay.

In the ABC's of mentoring, writer Bob Biehl defines mentorship in this way:

> "Mentoring is a lifelong relationship, in which a mentor helps a protégé reach her or his God-given potential. Mentoring explains clearly and completely what mentors do and don't do, the nature of the mentor/protege relationship, the most common roadblocks to effective mentoring, and more to help you succeed as mentor or protege.
>
> Mentoring is like having an ideal aunt or uncle whom you respect deeply, who loves you at a family level, cares for you at a close friend level, supports you at a sacrificial level, and offers wisdom at a modern Solomon level. Having a mentor is not like having another mother or father. Mentoring is more "how can I help you" rather than "what should I teach you?"[4]

---

[4] Biehl, Bob. "The ABCs of Mentoring." Lifeway.com. http://lfwy.co/2NjPjF3

75

Even though Yvette tried to make Rebecca believe she had it all together, in reality, she tried to forge ahead through parenthood, too. She was doing the best she could, and Rebecca saw it as an opportunity to have someone a little more knowledgeable about rearing black children in an all-white world help her along the way.

So, what if she hadn't taken Yvette's advice? What if she had stormed off, huffing and puffing at Yvette's strong remark, allowing her pride to guide her actions instead of her humility? What would have become of Randall then? Sure, Randall might have gotten along just fine. Maybe he would have been the successful weather commodities trader he had grown up to be. But what if they hadn't taken her advice about putting him in that private school so he could learn not only about life but how to be himself?

Mentoring Mimics Life More Than We Think

As I shared in the beginning of this chapter, I eventually found a spiritual mentor in a woman whom I would not have gravitated to otherwise. We were not the same age and didn't have the same things in common. I wouldn't have reached out to her in different circumstances. However, I met her at a book signing in a nearby town. We set up our tables near each other and hit it off when the lack of crowd interest forced us to find ways to pass the time. Although we live several hours away from each other, we kept in touch though social media.

As I came across Titus chapter two in the Bible, and my husband spoke about finding a "soul friend," I prayed about whom I could enlist that not only had some years of wisdom but also could help me both spiritually and professionally. Her name came to mind, so I approached her about mentoring. She suggested calling each other once a week, reading a book together, and praying for each other about our lives and our careers. It has been a year and a half since our first phone call, and I treasure those moments we talk. The calls only take a half an hour each week, but it's not about the time. It's about getting to know each other and investing in each other. That's what mentoring really is: investing in someone's life for his/her good and helping that person be the best he/she can be.

My soul friend wants what's best for me. I know I can call her at any time about just about anything. When I got a contract we had been praying about, I called her outside of our regular calling time. In fact, she was the first person I called. It didn't seem right not to tell her first. After all, whom else would I think of sharing that milestone with than someone who cared about me like a mother cares for her daughter? We weren't just calling each other just to pass the time or to say we did something; we had bonded. That's what mentoring does. It bonds you to the other person like nothing else does.

That day at the pool was a milestone moment, too. Rebecca thought they were going to pass the time and cool off on a hot summer day. Instead, she made a friend, a confidant, a cheerleader who wouldn't just watch from afar as Rebecca made mistakes but would walk alongside of her, put her arm around her shoulder, and share in Rebecca and Randall's milestones for better or for worse.

The moment I saw you, I knew you were my boy. You were not a choice; you were a fact. You were never a replacement, son. Do you understand?

Jack to Randall

Chapter Seven
Adoption into the Kingdom

In the movie *Lion*, Saroo, played by Dev Patel, goes on a search for twenty-five years for his mother.

When Saroo was five years old, he and his brother went to look for night work. His brother told him to stay on a bench and wait for him until he returned. Saroo, tired from the journey, fell asleep on the bench. When he woke up the next morning, Saroo is on a boat traveling thousands of miles to Calcutta and away from his mother and brother, unable to get back to them.

Despite Saroo's troubled childhood, a couple from Australia adopt him. A grown man and using modern technology such as Google Earth, he's able to find the small village in which he grew up. Returning there, he's reunited with his mother in a tearful reunion.

In an article entitled, "Why Every Christian Should See the Movie *Lion*," the author states, "*Lion* is a powerful film partly because it shines a harsh light on the cruel reality of poverty and child exploitation. But it is also powerful because it explores the beauty of adoption. Saroo's adoptive mother, Sue Brierly (Nicole Kidman), tells him she knew when she was a young girl that she would adopt a child from another culture.

One of the most moving moments in the film occurs when Saroo tells Sue he's sorry she and her husband, John, couldn't have their own kids. She gently scolds Saroo for thinking he was some kind of second-class substitute for a biological child. 'We chose not to have kids,' Sue says, explaining that she and John adopted Saroo and another Indian boy, Mantosh, because there were already so many children in the world who needed parents."[1]

Every Christian should be able to relate to Randall's story. We all have been adopted into the Kingdom of God. We are God's sons and daughters through Jesus' atonement on the cross. Following are some verses regarding adoption:

- "For he chose us in him before the creation of the world to be holy and blameless in his sight. In love he predestined us for adoption to sonship through Jesus Christ, in accordance with his pleasure and will—to the praise of his glorious grace, which he has freely given us in the One he loves" (Ephesians 1:4-6).

- "The Spirit you received does not make you slaves, so that you live in fear again; rather, the Spirit you received brought about your **adoption** to sonship. And by him we cry, 'Abba, Father'" (Romans 8:15).

---

[1] Grady, J. Lee., "Why Every Christian Should See the Movie Lion." Charismanews.com. http://bit.ly/2Nl4T3j

- "Not only so, but we ourselves, who have the first fruits of the Spirit, groan inwardly as we wait eagerly for our **adoption** to sonship, the redemption of our bodies" (Romans 8:23).

- "Theirs is the **adoption** to sonship; theirs the divine glory, the covenants, the receiving of the law, the temple worship and the promises" (Romans 9:4).

The disciples understood the value of adoption. Reeling from Jesus' death and resurrection, they didn't know what to think. Jesus made them the promise that He would send them His Spirit in His absence. But weeks had passed and still no Spirit. They started to get discouraged, but then the Spirit showed up:

"When the day of Pentecost came, they were all together in one place. Suddenly a sound like the blowing of a violent wind came from heaven and filled the whole house where they were sitting. They saw what seemed to be tongues of fire that separated and came to rest on each of them. All of them were filled with the Holy Spirit and began to speak in other tongues as the Spirit enabled them" (Acts 2:1-4).

What a transformation! Peter, a man who was best known for denying Christ in public, is now transformed and begins to heal those in neighboring towns and preaching to the crowds. When we receive the Holy Spirit, we are new people.

Randall wanted to have a new life, too. He wanted to fill the gap he had within his soul.

Although we have the love of our earthly parents, our souls still yearn to know our heavenly Father. Just like Randall desired to know his biological father, our souls feel incomplete unless we fill it with the knowledge of our Savior, which we are all invited to do by our Father's invitation. However, some people choose to reject that invitation.   When we reject that invitation, our souls still long to be filled. We fill it with temporal things in an attempt to bridge the gap between a distant God and a loving, intimate relationship with the Savior.

Alcohol, drugs, shopping, food, and exercise are all ways we use to fill that void. That's both for unbelievers and believers that never have experienced God's presence in a new way. *This Is Us* is not written from a Christian worldview, so Randall tries to fill his longings with perfectionism, possessions, family, and other things.

Author Pam Christian succinctly communicates the concept of adoption: "Those who choose to believe in God are predestined to be adopted into God's family through faith in Jesus. We are united to God, which is love, when we have repented of our sins and have accepted Jesus Christ as our Lord and Savior. His Holy Spirit is then given to us as guarantor of our adoption." She continues, "God not only forgives our sin but goes even further by adopting us into His family. This inheritance includes additional demonstrations of God's love including salvation, strength, hope, peace, comfort, providence, fellowship and so much more!" [1]

If I'm honest, I don't quite understand the concept of adoption. I came from a two-parent home, and I always knew who my parents were. Although I do believe the good relationship with my father contributed to the ease of which I am able to follow God, I don't know what it's like to not know who my biological father is. To prepare for this chapter, I thought it best to ask someone who has been through the adoption process. A gentleman in my former church, Jeff Wilcox, was adopted as a baby. It was not until he was much older that he began to wonder about his biological mother and father. He, in turn, adopted a child with his wife and reared him as his son.

I asked Jeff some questions about his thoughts and feeling surrounding the concept of adoption. He always knew from the time he was a child that he was adopted. He has a brother with whom he grew up, who was also adopted.

When Jeff attended college, he began to contemplate finding his birth parents. In December 1985, at the age of 25, his adopted mother passed away, which was the catalyst for him to begin his search. However, he got married and began a family of his own, so he lost the desire to search.

---

[1] Christian, Pam. *Revive Your Life: Rest For your Anxious Heart* (Protocol Publishing, Nashville: 2016). P.86-87.

Once his kids moved out of the house, the desire to search grew once again. He got to meet his biological half brothers and sisters. Sadly, his mother had passed away two years before that, and he never found his biological father. Ironically, all of his brothers and sisters knew he lived close to them but respected his privacy and did not pursue a meeting until he began to ask questions.

When I asked him about any feelings of abandonment he may have had from being adopted, he at first said no, but he did struggle with self-worth. Once he answered my question, his wife prodded him to explore his feelings in depth. He realized he also struggles with feelings of abandonment. He added that he didn't search for his biological parents earlier because he felt a sense of loyalty to his adopted parents and didn't want them to feel as though he was being disloyal to them by making them feel like they weren't enough.

I can see the same tension Jeff references in Randall as he figures out how to have a relationship with his father while not alienating his current family members. This is evident when Randall tells his children William is "just a friend who likes to have sleepovers" instead of their grandfather. He even hides the fact from his wife Beth that he had searched for him until he has actually located him. Then he brings him back to his home to stay without even telling her! Beth, the loving wife she is, takes it all in stride and allows him to stay, that is, not without asking him some poignant questions.

Beth asks him, "What are you doing here? Are you really sick?"

I imagine that might have appeared harsh to the audience, but she's trying to protect her family, including her husband. This is where she first reveals that Randall has mental health issues, a problem that becomes clear in a later episode.

Beth tells William, "Eight years ago I was pregnant for the first time. And Randall was vying for partner at his firm. We just bought this house on faith, even though it needed a lot of work. Even though we couldn't afford it whatsoever. Randall made partner, he did all the work on the house himself so that we didn't have to spend a penny, and he made sure I didn't lift a finger during my pregnancy. The problem is he stopped sleeping, and one morning when I was in the bathroom he called out to me, and he was confused, you know? He was confused because he couldn't see anything. My mountain of a man could no longer literally see anything through his eyes. His twenty-eight years of being perfect finally caught up to him that morning, and he pulled himself out of it. He self-corrected because that's what my man does. Randall is not free of vice. His vice is his goodness. It is his compulsive drive to be perfect. That's why I love him, but that is also why I have to protect him sometimes."

One of the many reasons why this show is heralded for great storytelling is because they address issues not normally dealt with on television. Much like another NBC hit *Parenthood*, it sheds light on panic attacks and mental issues in the same way *Parenthood* dealt with issues like breast cancer and autism. Superb acting from Sterling K. Brown and Justin Hartley who finds Randall on the ground completely incapacitated, it gives audiences a unique look into the life of someone who suffers from anxiety. From an article on Health.com:

"Anxiety is a mental health disorder, but the symptoms of a panic attack are very real. During Randall's present-day attack, he's shown shaking, sweating, hyperventilating, and having difficulty breathing." This was a pretty accurate portrayal," Dr. Murrough tells *Health*. "When you're experiencing a panic attack, it can feel like you're dying or losing your mind." The blurred vision that Randall experiences is also important: "The blurring of his vision gave the feeling of detachment or unreality," says Dr. Murrough. "De-personalization or feeling disconnected from your body is another common symptom of a panic attack."

Like my friend Jeff mentioned, I imagine Randall struggles with self-worth as well. From his brother never acknowledging him publicly as his brother to being different because of his skin color, Randall has to feel like he must prove himself to others to be worth something. He faces the additional pressure of not only being different but also being singled out as being more intelligent than his siblings. Thus, he faces even more pressure of more homework and feeling like he not only has to succeed, but he has to remain at the top of his class.

From vulture.com, author Maggie Fremont writes, "Kevin gears up for a big speech about feeling unsupported, but he's distracted by a giant billboard for *The Manny* featuring his replacement: a very handsome black man. When Kevin says, 'That's great. Replaced by another black man,' neither brother can hold back their real feelings. Kevin's always felt overshadowed by Randall. That's because he was black and adopted; their mother treated him as if he were more important. Randall counters: She had to treat him that way because Kevin treated him like a dog. And like a dog, Randall kept coming to Kevin for more. It was Kevin's love he craved the most." [2]

Favoritism and Adoption

In the episode, *The Best Washing Machine in the Whole World*, Randall and Kevin's sibling rivalry comes to light as they fight over whether or not Randall was favored. Randall finally admits, "Yeah, yeah. Mom favored me." This admission gives us a window not only into Kevin and Randall's relationship but also a window into Randall's soul.

As someone who is favored, it can actually cause the favored person to feel as though they have to keep themselves on top in order to find their place in the world. The pedestal they are placed on is high, and a fall from it can prove more bruising to the soul than a favorite would like to admit.

---

[2] Fremont, Maggie. "This Is Us Recap." Vulture. http://bit.ly/2RpmF8V

Favoritism is a familiar topic in the Bible as well. In fact, it's prevalent in one of the first stories in God's Word. It's interesting that the Rebekah in the Bible and Rebecca Pearson share some similarities and are the perpetrators of this sin in both situations (more on that later.) Rebekah, who wants Jacob to receive the father's blessing rather than his brother, Esau, hides his identity by dressing him in animal skins to imitate Esau's hairy arm. Rebecca in the sitcom hides the fact she knew about William throughout Randall's life and hid that fact from him until he was an adult. To make up for this loss, she favors him to make his life easier since his life has been difficult from the start.

Joseph of the Bible understood what it was like to be favored as well: "Now Israel loved Joseph more than all his children, because he was the son of his old age: and he made him a coat of many colors. When his brothers saw that their father loved him more than any of them, they hated him and could not speak a kind word to him" (Genesis 37:3-4).

Joseph wasn't shy about flaunting his new gift (or his favoritism) in front of his brothers. Tired of hearing it and allowing jealousy to reign, they steal Joseph's coveted robe, throw him into a cistern, and then sell him to some Midianite merchants. Talk about abandonment issues! Not only did they feel he wasn't even worth having as a brother, but they sold him for only twenty shekels of silver, a mere pittance for the life of a blood relative.

In his book <u>Soul Care</u>, Dr. Rob Reimer expounds on the sin of favoritism through the story of Joseph and his brothers. He writes, "Joseph was greatly affected by the family sin of favoritism. It wasn't just that his bothers hated him. He developed an attitude of pride, and he struggled with comparing himself and others. This is typical of someone who has experienced the sin of favoritism in his or her upbringing. They are competitive and comparative; they are always seeking to establish their pecking order, fearful that their place in life will be lost." [3]

God, in His wisdom allows Joseph to exercise forgiveness and to work through the deprivations in his soul from his brothers' abandonment. He blesses him immensely and He is able to reunite with his brothers and enjoy the gift of their fellowship. In the same way, Randall is blessed immensely too. He has a beautiful home, a lucrative job, and a loving, devoted wife. But those deprivations still remain.

In God's economy, though, Randall, can be adopted into God's kingdom, and so can we. No longer do we have to feel abandoned or have to prove our worth to anyone. Christ's death paid for our worth on the cross. Christ believed we were so worthy of life He gave up His life so we could have life in return. This is good news!

---

[3] Reimer, Rob. *Soul Care*. (Carpenter's Son: Nashville: 2016). P.59.

Déjà Vu?

As much as I don't understand adoption fully, Deja, the girl Randall and Beth take into their homes as part of the foster care system, does. A troubled girl, never knowing who her father is, is no stranger to trauma. Her mother, too busy being a teenager than a mother, leaves Deja with her grandmother throughout most of her toddler years. When Deja is a young child, her grandmother dies of a heart attack in front of her. Deja has to grow up quickly and take care of both herself and her mother.

"What would I do without you?" Deja's mom often says to her, placing an unnecessary burden on her.

Not only does Deja have to care for her mom, but she has to care for herself when she's placed in foster care after her mom leaves her home alone while at work. In and out of abusive homes, it's no wonder she is hesitant to trust Randall and flinches at his presence. Just as she begins to feel comfortable with them, her mom gets out of jail and comes back for her, only to be evicted from their apartment and forced to live in their car. Randall and Beth rescue them, and the mother flees for the final time, unsure she can give her the same life the Pearsons can.

The season finale of season two beautifully depicts Deja's struggle with her identity. Toby's mother, upon meeting Randall's daughters, says the two girls look like Beth, but Deja looks like Randall, sending Deja spiraling down into anger and resentment over her plight. Taking a baseball bat, she breaks the windows of her car and the other guests' cars at Kate and Toby's wedding.

What this means for déjà in future seasons is anyone's guess. Will she succumb to her anger and make the same poor decisions that will land her in jail as her mother, one can only guess. But the struggle to have a family is a struggle she will have for the rest of her life.

Randall comments, "You remind me a lot of myself."

We as an audience can see why. Much throughout Randall's childhood, Randall struggled to find his real parents. People who look like him roll their tongues like him and think like him. It was a struggle he had for his whole life, too, except he turned his angst into something positive using his intellect and anxiety to drive him to a successful job, marriage, and family. He rid himself of his feelings of abandonment and accepted His adoption by Jack and Rebecca.

By taking it one step farther, we Christians can also achieve intimacy with God by accepting our adoption into the Kingdom. But how do we do that?

Following are some ways we can be set free from feelings of abandonment and accept our adoption into God's kingdom:

1. Accept God's approval and love.

This is key. As Christians, we become God's children through Christ's death and payment for our sin. But if we are looking to prove our worth through our jobs, our relationships, or our possessions, we don't fully understand the significance of what Christ has done for us. When we can live each day walking in the freedom of our Father's love and approval of us, we don't worry about others' approval of us. We already have it. How freeing is that?

2. Unpack your soul baggage.

Just like Joseph had issues with love because of his brothers' treatment of him, Randall does, too. He lives in the reality that his brother Kevin doesn't acknowledge him as his brother, which causes him to overachieve and prove his worth. He launches into a panic attack because of the pressure of the realization that his mother hid his biological father from him all his life, plus the pressure of a new (and better) co-worker vying for the same account at work to Beth's mother's injury causing Beth to leave Randall to care for the girls and an ailing father, and the pressure of having to be perfect. If he had talked to a professional who could have helped him work through those soul issues, the panic attack might not have been an issue, but the stigma of needing professional counseling may have made him feel like a failure in life, leading him to ignore the life-giving help he could have received.

Christians have the beauty of fellowship with other brothers and sisters in Christ with a myriad of gifts, both

God-given and professional. As a Christian, determine to utilize the gifts of those around you.

Are there people who possess the wisdom that can help you sort through issues? Is there someone you trust who is bold enough to challenge you to let go of those feelings of abandonment and self-worth and trade them for feelings of freedom and acceptance, both of yourself and others' deeds to you? We need not feel embarrassed or ashamed to ask for help from our brothers and sisters in Christ. That's why we are one body—to help all of us function together properly so the Bride can unite with the Groom when He comes for all born-again believers.

I haven't been physically adopted, but I've been spiritually adopted into Christ's family as a daughter of the King. This is an opportunity afforded to all of us, but our worth cannot hinge on whether or not we have our physical parents in our lives or not. Rather, our heavenly Father waits for us to accept His love and unswerving invitation to be His favorite.

"You are Jack Pearson's son. You have him inside of you. And when you're nervous or at your most nerve-wracking moment, the curtain's about to go up, all you have to do is remind yourself of that, and you'll be fine."

Miguel

Chapter Eight
True Identity

All the characters, from Jack and Rebecca to the kids, are looking to find their worth and significance. Jack wants to be enough for his wife. Rebecca wants to discover something that fulfills her as her vocation, to break free from "just being a mom." Kate wants to be noticed for something apart from her weight. Kevin wants to find the love he lost when he divorced his wife. Randall is finding his significance in his job and his family to cover up the fact he wants to be loved and accepted.

We all want to be noticed. We all want to make an impact on the world around us. But if we place our worth and value on things other than allowing Christ to fill us, we will never find the significance we're looking for. Whether we think we're finding our self-worth or building our self-esteem, it's all a myth.

I surveyed some teens and asked them to define self-esteem and to explain its role in their lives. Following are the questions and some of their responses:

1. *What does self-esteem mean to you?*

   "A confidence—the ability to portray yourself how you want to be seen, not how others see you. You don't let what others think affect major decisions. It's more important what you think of yourself." ~ Heather K. Coudersport PA

2. *Do you think it's possible to have a high self-esteem all the time? Why or why not?*

"I don't think it's possible to have a high self-esteem all the time. For that to be possible, you'd have to never care what anyone said about you and not let it have a toll on how you think of yourself at all, but I don't think that is even humanly possible. Since everyone has the yearning to be accepted by people, they're going to feel bad about themselves sometime because no one is perfect—even if they have a high self-esteem most of the time." ~ Kasey C. Coudersport, PA

3. *Who are some people in your life that you think have a high self-esteem? What about them makes you think this is so?*

"Some of my close friends in church definitely have high self-esteem. Their focus is on God, and they know that they are beautifully and wonderfully made. This doesn't mean they're invincible. Words still hurt them, and they have days where they feel bad about themselves. But when they focus on what God thinks of them, what others think doesn't matter as much." ~ Hannah M., St. Paul, MN

4. *What things/ circumstances make your self-esteem plummet? What circumstances make it skyrocket?*

"My self-esteem plummets when my friends and family say something demeaning. I brush it off like it's no big deal, and they probably don't mean it, but when it comes from someone you love, it just hurts more and makes it all the more realistic. My self-esteem grows when someone compliments me on something that I'm not necessarily good at. For example, I stink at basketball, but my friends said I did really well even though I probably didn't." ~ Mikaela C. Wallingford, CT

5. *Do you think your self-esteem is based on what others think of you? Why or why not?*

"Yes, I feel like my self-esteem affects the way I present myself to people, especially in high school. They will judge you by your attitude and posture as well as your personality, so having high self-esteem will show people you have a positive attitude about yourself." ~ Natalie M., CT

No matter who you are, believer or unbeliever, we all have a need to feel good about ourselves, which is predicated by how much we feel we are loved and how we connect to others. But if we don't address our spiritual side, and accept the love and approval already given to us by a Savior who loves unconditionally, we will never find our identity in God but on people and possessions.

Author Robert McGee writes, "Whether labeled self-esteem or self-worth, the feeling of significance is crucial to man's emotional, spiritual and social stability, and is the driving element within the human spirit. What a waste to change behavior without truly understanding the driving needs that cause such behavior!"[1]

The God Who Sees

Recently attending a women's event, I registered at the welcome desk and stepped to the side.

"Please write your name on the nametag." The woman pointed as she slid a sticker toward me. I wrote my name in big letters and slapped it on my chest. I entered the auditorium and sat down in one of the front rows. I waited forty-five minutes before the event began, looking around while haphazardly looking at my phone. People filed into the seats in front of me and behind me, but no one said anything to me. I smiled at the people filing in, and they smiled back, but no one asked anything about me. No one asked who I was or where I lived. It was like I was invisible.

Before I pursued an intimate relationship at the age of eighteen with Jesus, my identity was wrapped up in how many friends I had, what designer clothes were on my body, and what grades appeared on my report card. But I soon learned that all those things don't define who I am. Christ's love does. Yet, identity is something every human struggles with throughout her life.

---

[1] McGee, Robert. *The Search for Significance.* (Houston: Rapha Publishing, 1990). P. 15.

Adam and Eve had identity issues, too. Genesis 2:19-20 says, "Now the LORD God had formed out of the ground all the wild animals and all the birds in the sky. He brought them to the man to see what he would name them; and whatever the man called each living creature, that was its name. So the man gave names to all the livestock, the birds in the sky and all the wild animals."

The animals and everything created up to this point had been God's. Yet, at that moment, He partners with Adam and gives him the sole responsibility of naming the animals. He allows Adam to identify with Him as a co–creator. What's Adam's first job? Giving the animals their identity through their names. Adam can truly identify with God through participating in His work.

We fight that tension as much today as Adam and Eve did back then. Kate, Kevin, and Randall certainly do. The world pressures us to identify with it when we act like it. But we choose to identify with God when we separate ourselves from the world through actions that please God rather than displease Him. However, we often serve and lead in churches to feed our own need for significance rather than living in the knowledge that our worth was settled on the cross long ago. When we don't fully understand and accept our Father's love, we look for other outlets to fill that need instead. We look for ways to fill the voids in our lives through counterfeit versions of wholeness.

All of us struggle with who we are and what our purpose on earth is. Even the first man and woman, Adam and Eve, struggled with their self-image. Before the fall, Adam and Eve accepted themselves for who they were. They were content with their love for each other as well as God's love for them. Being naked meant they were fully exposed before God and each other, and they were okay with it! There were no secrets, no reason to hide anything from each other. They knew one another fully, and nothing stood in the way of having the fullness of fellowship and intimacy God desired for them.

That all changed when Satan seizes the opportunity to capitalize on Eve's misinformation. Satan plants a seed of doubt into Eve's mind that maybe God was holding out on them. They assumed that perhaps being like God would be better than what they had already. Maybe God didn't have their best in mind like He had promised. Eve not only doubts God's unconditional love for her, but she doubts her love for herself, too.

Kate finds her identity in the number on the scale. Although weight loss would shrink her body size and also reduce her risk for major health issues like diabetes and cancer, she found a false sense of identity from her childhood. As seen in flashbacks, Kate and Jack have had a close bond. From Jack's speech to her being a princess at the community pool to striking a pose at her birthday party, Kate always believed her dad was a knight in shining armor. As she goes through her teen years, though, her romantic perception of Dad is replaced by desperate attempts to be the glue that keeps her mom and dad's marriage together. It's not until her exercise session at fat camp that we realize she has always blamed herself for her father's death.

Regardless of the reason, Kate's identity is one of guilt and shame. She lives her life bowed to the shame she feels of her role in her dad's death. This has definitely impacted her relationship with men.

Kevin's identity is also rooted in shame and guilt and looks for significance in his career—and not having great results. When Toby encourages him to find the person he can't live without, he gets back together with his ex-wife, Sophie, trading his identity as an actor for an identity as Sophie's significant other, that is, until Ron Howard offers him a job as an actor for a new play. Whether that decision ruins his second chance at love or not remains to be seen, but if he chases his dream of being a big actor, it will come at a cost, a cost he may not want to pay.

Randall's identity is also wrapped up in his job: coming in early, never being late, never calling out sick. He realizes that for the first time in ten years he needs some time off. With the impending responsibilities mounting on him, he is struggling to keep afloat in the weight of his duties. On the verge of a panic attack, he takes time to go on a trip to see William's hometown of Memphis. In the throes of grief from losing his father, his co-workers demonstrate they really don't know (or care) about Randall at all. Sending him a generalized card signed by "The team" and a case of pears (which he is allergic to), he begins to understand the magnitude of William's influence on his life. Randall begins to see what's most important in life and waltzes into the office, quits his job, and announces to his wife he wants to adopt a baby, a beautiful example of paying forward the love and sacrifice Jack and Rebecca had made for him.

Although Randall and Kevin seem to have nothing in common, they both have a warped sense of identity. Fighting over attention from their parents, seeking the approval they desperately crave, each look to their careers to find their worth, both of which come up empty. Although they may never fix their broken relationship severed over years of jealousy and anger, they will always have their desire to find significance in their work in common.

Author and Pastor Chuck Swindoll writes:

"Where do you find your significance? I mean, honestly, what is it that bolsters your sense of "worth" in this world. Is it your boat? Your grandkids? How about your expanding portfolio? If your dream home burned to the ground, would your sense of who you are as a person go up in flames with it? It's easy, isn't it, to let other things control our self-perception. As long as activities at work are humming along nicely, we feel great about ourselves. As long as the children are not in trouble with the law, and the tomatoes in the garden are ripening, well, as James Brown would sing, 'I feel good!' Yet we pay a high price for finding our significance in any thing or person other than Christ. Things and people fail us. Cars break down, work assignments go haywire, and children don't act as we wish. Placing your self-worth in anyone other than our Lord is risky business. Trying to build a sense of significance by banking on past accolades or future achievements pays low dividends."[2]

The Pearsons are plagued with doubts:

Rebecca doubts whether she is a good mother to her kids, telling Jack, "We are going to screw up our kids," and asking Kate, "Did I do this to you?" when she asks her if she pushed Kate to gain copious amounts of weight when she monitored her eating habits as a child.

Kate doubts if she's worth falling in love with or worth hiring for a job as she turns to see people chuckling and sneering at her when she dances with Toby at Kevin's agent party.

Kevin doubts he'll be anything other than a thirty-six-year-old, washed-up actor. "What if Manny is as good as it gets? What if I'm only Manny good?"

Randall doubts he can keep everything under control at home with William's failing health,

[2] Swindoll, Charles, R. "Our Worth in Christ." TS Voice. http://bit.ly/2xZoBgq

Beth's crisis of helping her mother after she fell and broke her hip, and attending his kids' various activities. Jack doubts he's "enough" as he turns to drinking once his kids pull away from him and begin to have their own lives. William doubts if he's worthy of redemption after flaking on his promise to his cousin to write more songs so their music career could take off as well as abandoning his son so long ago.

As you will find within the characters and themes of this book, this *is* really us because we all want to be known for something in life. Identity is the missing key to finding our worth in Christ. Following is what the Bible has to say about who we are:

- I am complete in Him who is the Head of all principality and power. (Colossians 2:10)
- I am alive with Christ. (Ephesians 2:5)
- I am free from the law of sin and death. (Romans 8:2)
- I am far from oppression, and fear does not come near me. (Isaiah 14:4)
- I am born of God, and the evil one does not touch me. (1 John 5:18)
- I am holy and without blame before Him in love. (Ephesians 1:4; 1 Peter 1:16)
- I have the mind of Christ. (1 Corinthians 2:16; Philippians 2:5)
- I have the peace of God that passes all understanding. (Philippians 4:7)

- I have the Greater One living in me; greater is He Who is in me than he who is in the world. (1 John 4:4)

It's so easy to forget who God says we are when we're constantly bombarded with billboards, TV shows, magazines, and other media outlets that make us believe we are not "enough." Commercials spend billions of dollars each year selling us items that tell us if only we had them, that would prove we are better, prettier, and smarter, feeding any other insecurity we have. Yet, the deep insecurities still linger. Buying these items does fill our needs and should for a time, but they never truly satisfy.

As Christians we have the opportunity to accept Christ's unconditional love and approval of us. Just as Randall revels in his father's statement that "you were never a replacement. You were my son. That's a fact," we can revel in God's love. God, like Jack, is holding our faces, gazing into our eyes, and telling us, "You are my son. That's a fact."

Our mother made sure you feel special every minute of every day so you didn't have to feel like the odd man out. If you hadn't been a part of our family, I could have been the star.

Kevin

Chapter Nine
Sibling Rivalry

"It doesn't end well for Cain and Abel, that's all I'm sayin'," Beth says to Randall after Randall revels in the fact he beat Kevin in a morning run.

"Yeah, so much less repressed. But if we were Cain and Abel, I'd be Cain, right? Because that's the one that won. right?" Randall quickly replies.

It's no secret that there is a rivalry going on between Kevin and Randall. They're two brothers who've been at odds with each other since they were kids. Both fighting for each other's attention, they're also fighting to get into each other's worlds.

Randall, a highly paid, successful individual can't come out from the shadow of his celebrity brother, "The Manny."

Kevin wants to be taken seriously and have the family and wife Randall has. Both successful in their own way, they still want what the other has. But in the episode "The Best Washing Machine in the World," we get a unique glimpse into their relationship. Kevin, in a word, is cool. He got all his friends to laugh when he impersonated Inigo Montoya from "The Princess Bride," while Randall had only three of the kids from his class attend his party.

When they were fifteen, Randall asks Kate, "Why does he hate me so much?" to which Kate replies, "He doesn't hate you. You both are just so intense with each other. Lighten up a little. Joke around a little more."

In a kind gesture, Randall brings Kevin a snack and drink in his new bedroom downstairs. Randall, secretly not wanting Kevin to be separated from him, makes a joke out of the amount of asbestos that will be in his lungs.

Randall says, "I just came to see your dungeon, I mean, your digs, Totally cool. In a couple of days you won't notice that funny mildew. I give it about two weeks before to have some major asbestos imbedded in your lungs."

Kevin snaps back, "Are you deaf? I came down here to get away from you. Get out of here."

A physical separation has finally come between the two brothers where an emotional one had been there for many years. As they go to dinner together as adults, they figure out that they don't know anything about each other's lives. Randall is out of touch with the world, offering to take a selfie for Kevin, to which Kevin says, "No, it's a selfie; I can do it."

As they sit and eat, Kevin has his friends stop by and say hello. Doting fans want to take pictures, and yet never once does Kevin give Randall any sort of attention. When the man who played "The Manny's" best friend stops at the table and wants to connect, Randall asks, "How do you know him?"

Kevin quickly realizes that Randall has not seen one episode of "The Manny." Although the competition between the two brothers is just a surface issue, there lies a deep emotional and mental separation from each other.

Just as Cain had jealousy for Abel because God looked favorably upon Abel's offerings to God and Cain didn't, so does Kevin look down on Randall because Randall got more of his father's attention than he did.

Randall, who idolizes his brother growing up, now doesn't have to be jealous of him because he got everything he ever wanted out of life, too.

Randall and Kevin were on competing football teams in high school. When Randall had tackled Kevin on a play, Kevin's anger grew. When Randall tackled him again in the midst of making a touchdown, they fought each other on the field, and both were thrown out of the game.

Now as adults, all the anger comes to a head. After Kevin can't tell Randall what Randall does for a living, Kevin sees a billboard for the New Manny, a black man.

"Replaced by another black guy," Kevin says tongue in cheek, which launches Kevin into a heated argument when he says Randall received preferential treatment because he was black and adopted.

While Randall quips that he had it tough and being black and adopted was already hard enough, Kevin isn't buying it. Kevin then goes a step farther and claims Rebecca favored him. "Our mother made sure you feel special every minute of every day so you didn't have to feel like the odd man out. If you hadn't been a part of our family, I could have been the star."

This heated exchange causes them to fight in the middle of the street in New York where Seth Myers and other stars gather around them.

Seth Myers says, "Kevin, are you all right? Do you want me to call someone?"

To which Kevin says, "That is my brother."

When everyone calms down, Randall says, "That's the first time you called me your brother."

When those deep wounds like what Kevin and Randall still harbor from their childhood, true freedom can never be reached. The angry words and gestures of anger just turn a heart cold. No longer was Randall kind to Kevin as he once was. Kevin never had to reciprocate that love and now, in his pain where his life is not where he wants it to be, he can't turn to his brother anymore. In an important scene, Randall finally puts Kevin's claims to rest.

"You are right," Randall tells Kevin. "Mom did favor me. She showered me with attention and took my side more times than not, and I ate every bit of it up. I ate it up like Kevin. You want to know why? Because the one person that I wanted to hear it from the most...."

As the seasons unfold, we get an even deeper view of the tensions that run deep between Kevin and Randall. As a young boy, Kevin had to make a choice between getting the approval of his friends or sticking up for his brother when they called him Webster. He chose his friends, and he continued to make the choice to get acceptance from his friends ever since.

It may seem as though Kevin is a terrible brother, but the consequences of that choice plus the other choices he has made that has led him to a life of despair and depravity are in and of themselves their own prison cell. Kevin keeps himself locked up in a cell of self-loathing and a search for significance even though he could forgive himself for what he had done and set himself free from his self-made prison cell.

Both Randall and Kevin chase after significance in similar ways. Both use their work as ways to gain the respect and approval they crave.

Randall works late night at the expense of his own family to provide them the life full of luxuries and possessions he believes they want. All of this collapses, however, when Randall comes to the startling realization that the company he has worked for ten years does very little to console him when his father passes away. Giving him a box of pears he is allergic to and a card signed by "the team" Randall wonders what all of that work was for as well. Like father, like sons.

The Roots of Despair Run Deep

We are made aware by the last episode that Jack is unhappy in his life as well. Desperate to give Rebecca the life she wants after overhearing her crying when she asks her family if she and Jack can move in with them when they first are married, he takes a job he doesn't like while sacrificing his dream of owning his own business. In his mind he believes it will only be for a couple of years before he can save enough money to make his dream a reality, but after ten years, he's still at the same job. Unhappy with the life he has created, he turns to drinking, much to Rebecca's disapproval.

Kevin, unhappy with his life, turns to meaningless sex and an affair.

Randall, trying to balance the mounting pressure on himself turns to acquiring wealth.

In an interview with creator Dan Fogelman, he made a comment about the long- standing difficulty between Kevin and Randall: "Yeah, I think it is a step in the right direction. It's a complicated brother relationship of these two alpha males who grew up in the same house at the same time at the same age. So there's no one particular incident that broke them, nor is there one particular

114

conversation that can fix it overnight. Not that it's inherently broken, but we've hinted at it from the beginning." In the second episode, Kevin says, 'I was not a very good brother to you, was I?' Randall says, 'No, you weren't.' So I think it's going to be a series-long arc for them in a way as they find their new normal."[1]

It's interesting that sibling rivalry is always rooted in jealousy and is always passed down from one generation to the next. Adam and Eve's choice led them to be separate from God in fellowship, forcing them to live life on their own. Cain hated Abel, and jealous of God's favor for him, killed Abel in cold blood. Jacob wanted Esau's blessing and tricked his dad into giving it to him rather than Esau. Joseph's brothers hated him because of their father's favor, so they sold him to some merchants and stole his new coat. Rachel and Leah, both Jacob's wives, were jealous of each other: Leah was jealous of Jacob's love for her; Rachel was jealous of the fact that Leah could bear his children. Because of a father's favor, jealousy reigns supreme. When jealousy is the focal point, both parties lose out on what he/she really wants - the unconditional love and approval of a parent.

The Sins of Pearson Forefathers

Although Cain and Abel are the earliest example of sibling rivalry, it might be best to examine what was going on with their parents. Adam and Eve had everything they

---

[1] Snierson, Dan. "This Is Us Creator Talks Beth's Discovery, Seth Meyer's Cameo." Entertainment. http://bit.ly/2Qxciib

could have wanted: fellowship with each other, intimacy with the Father, and all of their needs met. But Satan's temptation in the garden drove them to not focus on all that they *had* but focus on the one thing they *didn't* have: the tree of knowledge of good and evil. When they took their focus off God and on to themselves, their lives as they knew them collapsed. Instead of taking responsibility, they blamed each other. That coupled with an unrepentant heart were what caused God to resort to banishment. How God must have grieved when he said goodbye to them! Although Cain was ultimately responsible for his choices, he didn't have the best legacy handed down to him either.

Randall and Kevin had poor legacies too. Jack didn't have the best home life, so he functions out of the poor example he had: a verbally and physically abusive father. Jack dreams of owning his own business he may never realize. Dejected, he reaches for alcohol to numb his pain.

More than twenty-five times in the Old Testament, the Bible talks about punishing the children for the sins of the forefathers to the third and fourth generations. It's jarring to read these words and to think God would punish an innocent generation for something their parents have done, but *This Is Us* exhibits this idea beautifully in that we see the consequences of Rebecca's and Jack's decisions and how they impact their children as adults.

God may not be punishing Kate, Kevin, and Randall, but Jack's and Rebecca's choices have directly (and indirectly) impacted their way of thinking and their approach to the world.

As the seasons unfold, we'll see the effect Jack's death as well as Rebecca's sacrifice of her dream has on her life and her choosing Miguel as her mate, but for now, we know that major argument she has with Jack is the catalyst to the crumbling of what appears to be a fairy tale romance.

But is Rebecca completely at fault here? What little we know about her family, we know her mother ran around trying to appease her father, who sat staring at the television on Sundays watching football and demanding a beer. It's obvious from this flashback that her parents ascribed to the belief that "children should be seen and not heard," when her mother says, "you'll have to play somewhere else. Your father is trying to watch the game." Even with the poor relationship she had with her parents, she still falls in love and marries a man exactly like her father—consumed with sports and issues with alcohol that quickly becomes his downfall.

History truly does repeat itself.

So, how can Randall and Kevin not keep playing the same bad hand of cards but reshuffle the deck and be dealt a different hand?

Can Kevin and Randall repair a damaged relationship? From Randall's forgiveness he has extended to his own father who never had any role in his life, to forgiving his mother for keeping the identity of William a secret his whole life, Randall has the capacity to extend the same grace and mercy to Kevin as he has to the others.

Can Kevin do the same?

Jealousy always plays a role in sibling rivalry. Kevin is jealous of Rebecca's favoritism and Jack's constant attention. He had to find a way to separate himself from the jealousy and find a way to receive the attention he needs. Acting is his way to get the pat on the back and the applause he longs for. But as we know, that's only a temporary fix to the soul cravings and aches that remain once the applause stops and he steps off that stage.

Randall is beginning to understand that life is not about how much wealth or possessions he has or how perfect he is in life but what he gives back to others.

William has demonstrated this in his poverty and his willingness to take an interest in the people around him. Even Randall's mailman notices William is absent after he has died. If only all of us can boast of the impact we have in others simply by paying attention and taking an interest in the people God has placed in our lives on a daily basis.

Comparison and Sibling Rivalry

I understand the difficulty sibling rivalry can cause and the ripple effect its effect can have in a life.

I vied for my mother's attention and approval growing up when it was given to my sister. I wasted many years feeling like I didn't measure up in life because I focused on this loss of love. When I became a Christian at age eighteen, I yielded my life to Christ who wanted to be both mother and father to me, filling the void that lack of love gave me. It took me many years to let go of the loss of my mother's love and accept God's love and approval for me.

I may never fully understand the depth and breadth of God's love, but I'm getting there. Every time I choose not to focus on what others have but instead focus on what God has given me, I break free from the bondage jealousy can be in my life. I experience the freedom people like the woman at the well felt when I do this. How wonderful to tell others about Christ and break free from the worries of others' perceptions and thoughts are about me. I have tasted the true water Jesus offered her when I can stop worrying about myself and start focusing on extending the blessing I can be to others.

The Opposite of Jealousy is Contentment

Although Randall and Kevin are dissatisfied with their lives despite their fame and wealth, they both are desperately missing meaningful relationships in their lives. However, they can experience contentment by simply accepting the situation as a part of their reality. The apostle Paul said it best when he says, "I am not saying this because I am in need, for I have learned to be content whatever the circumstances. I know what it is to be in need, and I know what it is to have plenty. I have learned the secret of being content in any and every situation, whether well fed or hungry, whether living in plenty or in want. I can do all this through him who gives me strength" (Philippians 4:11-13).

Although verse thirteen is a familiar verse for many people, it's also one of the most misquoted and misused passages. It is easy to recite that I can do all things through Christ who gives me strength when things are going well. When all of our needs are met and we are not experiencing trials, it's easy to believe this. But what about when you have lost everything in your life? What about when you don't have enough money to pay your bills or meet your needs? It's more difficult to believe you can pull out of a troubling situation and that Christ will always give you the strength to pull through. But this verse was written in the context of experiencing contentment no matter what life throws your way.

The apostle Paul should know! Jailed, beaten, and in chains, he considered it all gain if it meant more people would know Christ because of his example. He even contemplated whether death or living a life in chains for Christ would be better!

Kevin would trade all of his fame for a second chance with his ex-wife, Sophie, the love of his life.

Randall realizes to honor his father's legacy, he must give back, and he plans to adopt a baby to pay forward the love his parents extended to him. By shifting the focus from themselves and what they don't have to taking joy and experience the everyday blessings in life, they can go from chasing the faulty beliefs that wealth and fame are the key to happiness to experiencing true joy and blessing the people around them.

This is Us teaches us about the true joys in life. Forgiveness and contentment are the keys to joy. Jesus came to give the hope of salvation that will allow us to break free from the nasty rut of jealousy and embrace the joy of being a blessing to others in their lives.

It's always going to be about the weight for me, Toby. It's been my story ever since I was a little girl. And every moment that I'm not thinking about it, I'm thinking about it. Like will this chair hold me, will this dress fit me? And if I ever get pregnant, will anyone ever notice? It's just at the core of who I am. It's just deep inside, and eight tequila shots can only mask that for a couple hours.

Kate

Chapter Ten
Kate and the Modern-Day Woman at the Well

It's a familiar story to most Christians.

A woman wracked with pain from previous relationships gone bad walks to the well in her town to draw water. Avoiding the disapproving stares of society at eventide, she ventures out under the blistering noonday sun to get to the well fully aware that not many people frequent the well at that time. To her surprise, someone is sitting at the well. Not just anyone, a Jewish man, with whom she was not allowed to mingle.

He begins talking to her as if he has lost his mind.

What will everyone think?

Then he asks her the most insane question: "Can I have a drink?"

Didn't he know?

Didn't he see?

Following is the story in case you aren't familiar (from John chapter four):

Now Jesus learned that the Pharisees had heard that he was gaining and baptizing more disciples than

John—although in fact it was not Jesus who baptized, but his disciples. So he left Judea and went back once more to Galilee.

Now he had to go through Samaria. So he came to a town in Samaria called Sychar, near the plot of ground Jacob had given to his son Joseph. Jacob's well was there, and Jesus, tired as he was from the journey, sat down by the well. It was about noon.

When a Samaritan woman came to draw water, Jesus said to her, "Will you give me a drink?" (His disciples had gone into the town to buy food.)

The Samaritan woman said to him, "You are a Jew and I am a Samaritan woman. How can you ask me for a drink?" (For Jews do not associate with Samaritans.)

Jesus answered her, "If you knew the gift of God and who it is that asks you for a drink, you would have asked him and he would have given you living water."

"Sir," the woman said, "you have nothing to draw with and the well is deep. Where can you get this living water? Are you greater than our father Jacob, who gave us the well and drank from it himself, as did also his sons and his livestock?"

Jesus answered, "Everyone who drinks this water will be thirsty again, but whoever drinks the water I give them will never thirst. Indeed, the water I give them will become in them a spring of water welling up to eternal life."

The woman said to him, "Sir, give me this water so that I won't get thirsty and have to keep coming here to draw water."

Jesus knew her story all too well. Common to most women of her caliber in that day, she was looking for love in the all the wrong places. As she struggled to find the love and approval she had wanted in her marriages, she decides marriage was not for her. She didn't even bother to marry her newest beau. After all, it would only end up in anguish, right? But she doesn't know who's sitting at the well.

But He knows her.

It's interesting that the woman at the well has no name. Is it because she is not important enough to be named or is it something else? Is it because any one of us can insert our own names into that scenario and still have it apply?

Kate sure could. Wracked with guilt from her father's death—a death she blames on herself—she goes through life not running from man to man but to food to bury her feelings. This is nothing new, however. Her real "food issue" begins at that fateful day at the swimming pool. Kate, not even aware that her weight is a real issue for anyone (except for her mom, who in an effort to help Kate watch her weight, tells her to "eat all the grapefruit" while her brothers get sugary cereal to eat.) The issue of body image and weight become a struggle from that swimming pool day forward, an issue as she grabs her mom's sweater from the closet and notices the "S" imprinted on the inside tag and compared it to her "XL" one on hers. It becomes apparent as she goes to fat camp for a week in an attempt to lose the weight only to be thrown out because she has an argument with the camp owners' son. Her weight is also an issue as she breaks up with Toby because losing the weight has taken over every aspect of her life, robbing her of happiness and joy in the realization that her body does not define who she is.

In an article in "People Magazine," real-life Kate Chrissy Metz's life parallels Kate's in eerie ways. "A size 12 at the time, Metz followed her then manager's advice to lose 50 lbs. But when she moved to L.A a year later, the aspiring actress fell into a 'soul-crushing' 10-year spiral of weight gain and depression. With auditions for women her size ('I'd be getting maybe two auditions per year, and I'd always see the same small group of girls'), Metz thought, "Maybe I'm not tough enough, maybe I'm not good enough," she says. "I'd call my mom saying, 'Maybe I should just teach preschool.'"[1]

Whether she's carrying water home or auditioning for a new acting role, aren't both the woman at the well and

---

[1] Beard, Lanford. "This Is Us Chrissy Metz on Finding Happiness After Years of Dieting and Depression: 'I'm Proud of Who I Am'." *People* http://bit.ly/2QwBw04

Kate's worth and value wrapped up in someone else's perception of who they really are? In a sense, her dad Jack is her "Jesus"—constantly reassuring her that she's beautiful and special in every way as in the scene when her father talks to Kate in a stunning monologue about wearing the "magic shirt" that got Rebecca to marry him.

But hope in someone else's perception only takes us so far, doesn't it? In a poignant scene at Kate's eleven-year-old Madonna-themed birthday party, Jack tries to get Kate to cheer up when all of her friends want to go over to Kevin's party instead of hers by asking her to teach him how to Vogue. After they "strike a pose" for a few minutes, Kate's attitude suddenly turns downcast.

"I think I just want to be alone," Kate says to Jack.

Jack, realizing that his daughter is growing up and not needing his advice as much anymore, Jack dejectedly walks away.

And alone Kate stays. For most of season one we never see Kate have any friends (including long-time friend Sophie) outside of her brother Kevin, a relationship of which almost jeopardizes her relationship with Toby. "We are twins. Kevin will always come first. It's just the way it is," tells Toby.

The crutch of food that she leans on after her father's death only temporarily keeps her feelings of deep grief and sadness at bay. Letting it all out as we watch Kate let out a primal, guttural scream during her drum-inspired yoga session at fat camp, the audience understands that although Kate puts on a brave face, she is anything but healed. Kate has been hiding just like the woman at the well, just in a different way. Hiding from the world's disapproving glances is evidenced in episode two when she attends Kevin's Hollywood party and sheepishly dances with Toby for all the partygoers to see. She also hides from letting her heart experience the first real true love relationship since her father's passing during her tender teen years. It's like both the woman at the well and Kate have been living in a jail cell, but only Jesus and self-acceptance hold the key to their release.

Loneliness and the Woman

We don't know the reason behind why the woman had so many husbands. Some argue they had all died, giving this woman some form of dignity, while others propose she left them all, heaping more shame on her than she already carried. I can imagine the bucket she used to carry water to and from the well was already heavy, but to heap shame on her made the weight of that bucket, seemingly, unbearable.

She carries so much more than just an empty bucket. She comes wanting physical water—but the spiritual water she drinks freely from by the end of the conversation satiates her thirst so much more. No longer is she the social outcast, forced to remain quiet because her baggage renders her mute. Her interaction with Jesus offers her the opportunity to loosen her tongue and receive the joy for which her heart longed. Why else would she run among the towns' people proclaiming, "He told me everything I ever did!"

In His encounter with the woman at the well, Jesus broke three Jewish customs: first, he spoke to a woman; second, she was a Samaritan woman, a group the Jews traditionally despised; and third, he asked her to get him a drink of water, which would have made him ceremonially unclean from using her cup or jar.

This encounter shocked the woman at the well and transforms her life.

A man transforms Kate, too. When she meets Toby at an overeaters' group therapy meeting, she tells him, "I can't fall in love with a fat person right now." She puts her weight loss in front of everything in her life; yet, the loss of a man's love (her father) contributed to her weight issues in the first place.

The woman at the well gives up on love altogether (we can assume she's tired of losing all of the men before her last one, whom Jesus claims is not her husband.) Then she regains it on an ordinary noonday.

Toby transforms Kate, although she doesn't realize it at first. Treating her like a queen, he literally rolls out the red carpet and treats her like a rock star as he books a gig at the nursing home where his aunt lives. After a beautiful rendition of "True Colors," Kate has renewed her faith in men and in herself.

After a tryst in the nursing home supply closet, though, we realize Kate is not ready to give herself totally to love. After a phone call from her brother Kevin, she runs to him, leaving Toby behind. After a brief break up, Toby comes to see her at Christmas time, only to collapse on Randall's living room floor. The event changes Kate's perspective on the important things in life. One event, one ordinary day, can change a life. It did for the woman at the well and it did for Kate, too.

Taking Risks

The woman at the well took a risk running to tell the whole town about Jesus. As a woman who already was branded a whore, telling everyone about her encounter with a Jew might have made things even worse. How ironic that she tells everyone about a man even though in society's eyes she could never keep that man, any man, in the first place. She risked even more of her reputation by telling everyone whom she has met.

The Pharisees could have believed she had just found another man and could have taken bets on how long this new relationship would last. People in society probably would have branded her as a liar. After all, she didn't even have a man right now. Had she turned to prostitution by finding another one?

Her reputation in the town was shaky at best. Yet, Jesus chose to reveal himself to her.

Kate's life is similar because she has trouble trusting men too. She had friends who said they were embarrassed to be seen with her.

As season one unfolds, we assume she has had men dump her or mock her for her weight and make her feel worthless. Toby is the first one who hasn't been bothered by her weight and sees her just for her. Like Jesus, she has a knight in shining armor who has swooped in to save the day. But placing her trust in Toby is a big risk, too. Not only does she risk being dumped again; she also risks this person who also struggles with weight from derailing her plans to finally get hold of the one thing she hasn't struggled with in her life.

Temptation

The temptation for Kate is that she's constantly being dissuaded from keeping on track. First her weight is becoming a struggle as Toby has decided to stop dieting and eat what he wants, posing a distraction to Kate. But then the owner of the fat camp's son tempts her by flattering her and telling her that he's interested in a one-night stand. Although Kate is smart enough to tell the guy off, which ultimately gets her kicked out from fat camp, she finally takes a stand and doesn't let temptation keep her from keeping Toby at the forefront of her life. In the same way, she stays the course of her weight, even contemplating gastric bypass as a way to give her the push she needs. After getting a flight to see Randall and the family for Thanksgiving, she has a scary moment of plane turbulence, forcing her to reevaluate her life's choices thus deciding to do the weight loss surgery to potentially change (and save) her life.

Jesus was the "bypass surgery" for the woman at the well. She now no longer had to keep making bad choices that derailed her from success. One encounter with the Master and she reevaluated her life choices. She was set free and became passionate about telling others about that freedom of which they all could partake.

Moving Forward

The interesting thing to note about the Bible story is the woman, terrified of anyone seeing her or judging her for her life choices, is now shouting through the town about Jesus. But it wasn't until she dealt with her "stuff" that she was able to break free from her past and live in freedom in the future.

Kate has the same opportunity the day of her wedding. As she dreams of her parents' vow renewal, she tells Rebecca, who in turn asks, "And where is Toby in this dream?"

Kate realizes he's not pictured in it because she doesn't love him. Jack has taken center stage in her heart and she needed to let go of his influence in her life as well as her guilt, feeling she was responsible for his death. (He wouldn't have gone back into the house for the dog if it hadn't been at Kate's insistence.)

In order to move forward, the woman at the well had to go backward. Jesus identified her past failed relationships to help the woman understand who He was. He wasn't just a prophet or even a good guy; He was the one person who could give her what she truly needed.

Kate had to do the same as well. She had to let go of her dad as the main male relationship and set her sights on Toby, allowing him to fill the void her father had left.

In the scene at the reception, Kevin delivers a fabulous wedding toast. He explains that they have all been holding on to Jack's memories for too long, and they need to just breathe. The Pearsons take in a collective breath and breathe it out, letting go of guilt, pain, and perceived failures.

Perhaps you are holding onto guilt, pain, and failures, too. Do you need to take a breath and release all that you've been holding onto?

Following are two ways God can use your struggle with love and acceptance to impact the kingdom:

1. **Redefine your past** - Come to grips with what you have done. If you have a shady past, accept it. There's nothing you can do to change it, so why dwell on it? What is it about your past (your story) that's holding you back from being seen by the world or shouting from the rooftops about who God is?

Kate has a secret in her past, too. She blames herself for her father's death. Whether she was directly or indirectly involved remains to be seen. But either way, the guilt is spilling into every area of her life. It's also causing her to distrust men and herself whenever she gets into a serious relationship. Her distrust is causing her to miss out on the great opportunities of what might come her way.

However, at the season finale, Kate takes a leap of faith. She begins to see herself for what she really is: worthy. Thanks to Toby, she decides to pursue her singing career, taking over where her mom's career left off. With her great voice, that decision will surely catapult her into having a great career. But she can also make amends and serve her penance for the damage she believed she caused by encouraging her father to visit Rebecca while on tour, a decision that Jack ruins in his drunken state causing Rebecca to quit singing for the rest of her life.

2. **Confess your sins** – It's only through repentance and acceptance of what we have done that can God use us. We can't live in the light like First Timothy says if we haven't brought into the light what we have done. Confess it to someone.

Jesus disarmed the woman at the well when He told her about her sins, and He can do the same for us. He knows our sins; He just wants us to acknowledge them.

Allow the transformative work God does in your life to allow you to impact the Kingdom. Once you feel like you are free from all that baggage weighing you down, what's stopping you from doing His work? What might God be calling you to do now that you're free? Everyone has a purpose; we just need to find out what it is and not run from it, but do it.

Toby wants Kate to open up to him. That's why he postpones the wedding. He wants her to open up and talk to him about anything. Until she can talk about the one area of her life that causes her the biggest amount of shame (We know this from her primal scream in the middle of her exercise class), she and Toby will never be as close as a husband and wife should be.

As Christ dictates, we have to walk in the light in community. When we keep sin and shame a secret, it gives the devil a foothold. Confessing that openly will shed light on the areas where Kate still feels shame and push her to forgive herself for her past mistakes. It may not be easy, but with a strong community and walking in light by facing our doubts and fears can bring us the peace and significance we are all looking for.

I almost drowned! Do you even care? I tried to get to the deep end, but you never watch me. Don't touch me! You're so busy making sure that Kate's not eating too much and Randall's not too adopted, and meanwhile where's Kevin? Oh. Guess what? He's dead!

Kevin

Chapter Eleven
Kevin and the Modern-Day Solomon

On the surface, Kevin seems like the most shallow and superficial of the three kids. As the star of the fluff comedy "The Manny," Kevin wants to be seen as a serious actor and take his talent as an artist to the next level. However, his chiseled physique and celebrity status lends himself to be viewed more as a sex symbol than that serious actor he so desperately wants to be.

We know little about Kevin and his background, but what we do know tells us he has been desperate to be noticed all his life. We begin the series with Kevin telling two beautiful women, "You know where it all went wrong for me? It was 1986. They were sending the Challenger in space. Do you remember the Challenger? Christa McAuliffe. She was going to be the first teacher in space, right? She was going to change the world. I don't know how, but at least in second grade you could feel that. The middle of the school day the teacher brings in a TV. We're all sitting there watching the launch, right? We're all just sitting there. A bunch of seven-year-olds just watching and then *boom*! The whole thing just explodes. Little pieces of sweet Christa McAuliffe all came raining down on the state of Florida. It was awful. Maybe that was when I realized trying to change the world just leads to being blown up into little pieces all over Florida. Maybe that's how I wound up as 'The Manny'."

There is a yearning in Kevin's heart from the beginning of the show to want to do more and be more. On the set of "The Manny," after saying a silly line about breastfeeding a baby, he realizes that he is nothing in the acting world.

His director says, "Kevin, I know you care about the character, and I also know that you are a thirty-something actor whose biggest role previously was a three-episode arc on Nashville. So say the line or find another job. Because believe me when I say that I'll have you replaced by Ryan Gosling, Ryan Reynolds, or any other handsome Ryan faster than the time it takes for you to get to your car. Trust me, my ratings will go up."

Kevin, fed up with the trying to make everyone laugh like a puppet on a string, loses it on the set to the wide eyes of the audience (and a few cell phone video cameras, too.)

After a gripping scene with actor father Alan Thicke, he hugs the producer, who then tells him he needs a lighter version and to lose the shirt because it's better without the shirt." Kevin speaks to the audience: "Don't be alarmed, because it's not a real baby. This baby can't feel a thing because it's all fake." Taking Thicke's suitcase, he opens it to find it is open.

"Where ya goin,' Alan Thicke," Kevin asks, "and what are you going to wear when you get there?" He then turns to the writer and says, "It's not your fault, Daniel; it's not the writer's fault that the show is so bad, and it's so bad. It's not the network's fault for airing it. It's you guys," he says, turning to the audience. "I knew what this show was when I took it. Shame on me for taking the money, and shame on you for making me famous. Shame on all of us."

Although we are introduced to him as being a seeming playboy, known for sleeping with the actresses that play opposite him in the Broadway play for which he auditions, it's obvious he's desperate to give his life meaning. He's searching for true love, which we discover later on in the season that he already had true love with his ex-wife, Sophie, who is Kate's childhood friend and whom he cheats on and divorces. It's obvious he's been chasing after something that's been right in front of him the whole time.

Born to Make an Impact

Kevin has a desire to change the world and wants to make a difference. From his near drowning at the community pool in a desperate attempt to get his father's attention to his non-commitment to women, Kevin wants for people to know him for who he is, not for what he can do or what television show he is on.

In the episode, "Three Sentences," Kevin befriends Toby and shows him around New York City. However, we quickly learn that Kevin is known in New York, but not for being a good guy. After spotting two women on the street, Toby would like Kevin to introduce him. But Kevin's remarks define exactly who he is: "Whatever conversation I'm going to have with those girls, trust me, I've had, like, a million times before. It goes like this: "You watch "The Manny?" Really? Yes, the baby is cute in real life. Oh, you want to get into acting, too? Phenomenal! Margarita, Tequila soda, tequila on the rocks, tequila shot, hotel sex, room service, shower sex."

Toby then replies, "I can't believe we are in the same species."

What seems like a lifestyle full of carelessness and whimsy sounded good for a while for Kevin when he first got into acting. He can get any girl he wants and all the alcohol he can handle, night after night, with meaningless conversation after meaningless conversation, leading to meaningless relationship after meaningless relationship. It all seemed great…way back then.

It's also leads to a meaningless life.

In the same episode, we also see a glimpse of Kevin's first taste of acting. Standing on the coffee table, he recites the line from "The Princess Bride," the popular movie at the time.

"My name is Inigo Montoya. You killed my father, so prepare to die," Kevin says in his best Mandy Patinkin impression, which causes all the guests from Kate and Kevin's party to erupt in laughter. Finally, he is seen and accepted. It's no wonder he wants to chase after that the rest of his life. Acting fills a void for him. That is, until his failures from the past bubble to the surface.

In season two, his scene with Sylvester Stallone on the set of Kevin's movie sends him to a place of weakness. During a war scene, Kevin hurts his knee, forcing him to take pain medication to which he becomes addicted, combining it with alcohol. He relives his greatest nightmare: receiving an award from his former high school. As he steps out onto the football field, he remembers that night of his senior year when he hurt his knee, ending his football career, and, in turn, destroying his chances of a football scholarship. Thinking he's too good for community college, he never attends, making him feel stuck. His addiction also ruins his relationship with Sophie, his ex-wife, with whom he is working to reconcile their relationship. Instead of dealing with his pain, he numbs it with alcohol, drugs, and loose women, simply because he still seeks the approval of the world instead of believing he is enough exactly the way he is.

Like Father, Like Son

It's easy to see the parallels between Kevin and his dad.

Jack wants another baby with Rebecca after the kids reach the tender age when his influence and presence in their lives is quickly diminishing, but Jack struggles with being enough, just like Kevin.

141

It's evident Kevin is similar to Jack when he asks him, "My hair is cool, right, Dad? It's doing its thing?" It's evident when he stands at his Sophie's door and says the following monologue (perhaps the biggest acting job of his life):

> "Before you say anything, there are three sentences I need to say to you. I was head over heels in love with you the moment that I saw you, and I should have never let you get away. You were a part of me, like you were my arm, and when I lost you, it was like I lost my arm.... It's like I have been walking around without an arm for the past decade, and I really want my arm back because I never stopped thinking about it, not ever. (You look amazing, by the way.)" At the core of Kevin's being, there is a good man. But the lures of wealth and prestige and the deep ache within his soul to be known is more than he can resist.

The Charmer

"I really need to talk to you. I came here to beg you to come to opening night of my play," Kevin pleads with Mr. Novak, the critic.

Mr. Novak says, "I think that you choked. I think that without five takes and a laugh track that you know, you're nothing more than a playboy with no talent."

142

He charms the critic into attending the redo of his opening night, but he's surrounded by people who constantly tell him he's nothing more than their puppet, bought and owned by his agent and "The Manny's" producer. They make it obvious they don't care about him, only about the amount of money his TV show is making. Chewed up and spit out by the world, Kevin is searching for meaning in life.

King Solomon knew a bit about that search for meaning too. He had everything he could have dreamed of—power, prestige, women. He loved it…for a while. Until he began to search for more:

I said to myself, "Come now, I will test you with pleasure to find out what is good." But that also proved to be meaningless. "Laughter," I said, "is madness. And what does pleasure accomplish?" [3] I tried cheering myself with wine, and embracing folly—my mind still guiding me with wisdom. I wanted to see what was good for people to do under the heavens during the few days of their lives… I denied myself nothing my eyes desired; I refused my heart no pleasure. My heart took delight in all my labor, and this was the reward for all my toil. Yet when I surveyed all that my hands had done and what I had toiled to achieve, everything was meaningless, a chasing after the wind; nothing was gained under the sun" (Ecclesiastes 2:1-3; 10-11).

Solomon states that once you've achieved all the false promises the world claims to deliver, the heart always wants more. Now that Kevin has achieved the fame and celebrity status, his heart wants more. It wants to know and be known. He wants to love completely and fully, trading in meaningless one-night stands for intimate relationships. So, he chases after his ex-wife, whom he cheated on twelve years ago, to try to rekindle what he has lost.

An article on "Entertainment Tonight" online interviews Justin Hartley about his character Kevin. Hartley says, "The show's layered way of presenting its male characters has also impacted his views on masculinity and fatherhood. "It's reinforced a lot of things I thought before. One of the things I constantly do is try to show my daughter what that is, what that means, and what a man does," Hartley explains. "I try to show her that by example. I want her to find somebody that obviously measures up— she's wonderful—and who deserves her. And there obviously isn't anyone that does, but we'll get close, hopefully."

The themes on *This Is Us* are especially interesting for Hartley, who's not afraid to be vulnerable. "There's a time and a place where [being] a father is important, or being a brother, or having a relationship with a buddy," he says, "or what it is to be a man." [2]

This Is Us is helping audiences redefine all areas of their lives. It helps them define what forgiveness looks like,

[2] Lamb, Stacy. "Justin Hartley Brings Honesty and Humility to 'This Is Us'." ETonline. https://et.tv/2ICUQGd

what fear looks like, what struggle looks like, and helps them understand these areas are present in everyone's life.

It's your response to it and how it shapes your life that matters.

As Kevin moves into adulthood, we see him making better decisions once he has figured out what's important. He goes after the new movie Ron Howard is directing without a "what if I'm not good enough," attitude, but with an "I do have talent, and that is enough" one.

Jack's Death Has an Impact

As revealed in the "Three Sentences" episode, Jack dies during the kids' teen years. Teens need their dad during the teen years more than any time. Not having a dad during those tumultuous teen years forces the kids to navigate through life without a male adult to help them find their way. Since we know Kevin struggles with being known and seen, that ache is only magnified by the finality of never getting his father's attention. When he was ten, he asked his father to build model airplanes together. Although his father said, "Later," it's evident "later" never comes.

When Kevin's a teenager, he's in the middle of talking to his mother and father about his deepening relationship with Sophie, and Randall comes down in a panic about an assignment for school. His father ignores Kevin to take care of Randall. This creates jealousy within

Kevin because Randall always got the attention. Craving that same attention, he secretly resents Randall, causing them to drift apart.

In a scene where he calls Randall for the first time in years, Kevin asks for Randall's help on getting out of his contract from "The Manny."

"So, you are calling to ask what I think?" Randall asks.

"You know me, Randall, I care what everyone thinks."

This scenario gives us a sense that Kevin is a slave to others' perceptions of him and that approval (or disapproval) follows him into adulthood, allowing him to make choices based on others' perception of him. Instead of having his dad to believe in him, it is now Sophie's turn to believe in him. This is the missing piece to his puzzle, a filling of that void that's been filled with rejection. Now he has a new lease on life.

Or does he?

The turning point for Kevin comes in the episode "Jack Pearson's Son." Kevin, insecure about his ability to perform well in the play, goes to his mother's house but only encounters Miguel, (Rebecca's new husband and Jack's best friend).

Kevin finds an unlikely cheerleader in Miguel, a man who claims Kevin doesn't like, who says to Kevin, "You remind me of him. The way you move your arms, the way you talk. Sometimes you remind me of him so much that when I see you, the hair on my arms sticks up. Because when I'm around you, it's like I get a little piece of my best friend back. You are Jack Pearson's son. He is inside of you. So when you are at your most nerve-wracking moment and the curtain is about to go up, all you have to do is remind yourself of that and think about what he would do, and you'll be fine."

When the curtain is ready to go up, Kevin takes Miguel's advice. Instead of making his play debut as a serious actor, he does what his father would have done. He runs to Randall's side who has had a nervous breakdown at his job. Instead of berating him for not being there for him, he simply sits by him, takes him in his arms and holds him. It is a beautiful moment between brothers. Finally, there are no more walls erected to keep each other out when Kevin offers a gesture to tear those walls down.

Robert K. Johnston, author of Useless Beauty, says this about comparing movies and Ecclesiastes together: "Movies function as modern-day parables, giving us fresh eyes to see and ears to hear. Conversely, the paradoxes and tensions found in Ecclesiastes can provide interpretive lenses for the viewing of movies. The conversation is most productive and vibrant if it is two-way. Movies and biblical text can provide mutually penetrating perspectives on how viewers and readers hold on to the themes of despair and joy concurrently. This mutual conversation holds the promise of helping us celebrate "all this useless beauty."[3] Through modern day film (and TV as well) we see ancient biblical text come alive in a new way. The Bible has been around for years; yet, we see it reproduced in characters from television all the time. In fact, in the television show *Lost!*, there are rich parallels between the Bible and the characters of the show.

In The Gospel According to *Lost!*, Chris Seay writes, "If ABC's *Lost* and Coldplay's versions of *Lost!* sold sixteen million downloads on iTunes alone, then it's hard to imagine another story about lostness capturing a greater market share or reaching a higher acclaim. But Jesus seems to be the first storyteller to captivate large audiences (say seventy-five billion?) with a series of stories all about this abject quality of being missing or adrift or just plain lost."[4]

Seay continues, "In Luke chapter fifteen, Jesus masterfully wove together three stories: One told of a lost sheep, another of a lost coin, and finally, most profoundly, a lost son. In the midst of signs and miracles and stories about the kingdom, Jesus seems to break from the script

---

[3] Johnson, Robert K. *Useless Beauty: Ecclesiastes Through the Lens of Film.* (Baker academic; 2004). P. 32.

[4] Seay, Chris. *The Gospel According to Lost.* (Thomas Nelson, 2009). P. 95.

when he began this succession of stories. What could have prompted such a radical departure?" [5]

If television is a reflection of culture, then what does *This Is Us* reflect? It really is us in that we are all truly lost without Christ, and Kevin is no different. He is fumbling through life aimlessly wandering, grasping for whatever is familiar and real. He hopes if he grabs onto Sophie, that familiar person will anchor him and give him the direction he needs.

But putting faith in a person rather than in God is a recipe for disaster. People let us down. People leave when they get disappointed. And when they do this, we fumble toward other things that will satisfy. In this case, it is Kevin's divide between being taken serious as an actor to having work that brings him purpose and holding onto the love of his life. Grabbing onto either in an effort to find something that satisfies is always a shaky foundation.

---

[5] Ibid.

You're adopted, and we don't talk about that enough. Because to me, you are every part my son. And maybe I don't want you to feel like you stand out. But I need you to know something. I want you to stand out. I want all of you to be as different as you can possibly be, in all the best ways. I love you as much as a human heart can, kiddo. You are an exceptional young man. So don't let your old man's poor choices make you feel afraid to be different, OK?

Jack

Chapter Twelve
Randall and the Modern-Day Eldest Brother

In the show *Long Lost Family*, two hosts Janice Joyner and Chris Evans reunite adults and children with their biological family members who gave them up for adoption. The stories are heart wrenching, and the reunions would make even the strongest person shed a tear. What's interesting is that when asked how they feel toward their biological family, all of the adoptees say they're not angry with their parents for giving them up. In fact, some have even stated they're grateful to have been raised with such loving and kind people. Yet the biological family is often wracked with guilt and remorse over their decision. The reunion often brings closure to the person wanting to meet their biological family, and the family member often experiences peace when reuniting with their family members after so many years.

The Story is Key

Randall is very much like the eldest brother in the parable of the two sons. He's the one grumbling in the field, ungrateful for all the love he had from a great father all throughout his childhood. No matter how much love he had, he wanted more.

Adopted kids often have a yearning to find out more about their heritages to find out who they are most like, what traits they have inherited, and so on. Randall gets that in William, and in a way, gets to have a second father after his adoptive father Jack passes away when Randall was a teen.

In the Bible story, the eldest brother gets a second chance at the father's love, too. The eldest brother ignores the father while his brother is away, yet is envious once the brother returns and steals what he thinks is supposed to be his. Instead of welcoming his long-lost brother home after a time away, he gets angry and resents his brother and, ultimately, his father for his seemingly unfair treatment:

> "Meanwhile, the older son was in the field. When he came near the house, he heard music and dancing. So he called one of the servants and asked him what was going on. 'Your brother has come,' he replied, 'and your father has killed the fattened calf because he has him back safe and sound.' "The older brother became angry and refused to go in. So his father went out and pleaded with him. But he answered his father, 'Look! All these years I've been slaving for you and never disobeyed your orders. Yet you never gave me even a young goat so I could celebrate with my friends. But when this son of yours who has squandered your property with prostitutes comes home, you kill the fattened calf for him!' 'My son,' the father said, 'you are always with me, and everything I have is yours. But we had to celebrate and be glad, because this brother of yours was dead and is alive again; he was lost and is found'" (Luke 15:29-32).

Randall is the good kid. He's the boy next door. He's the person most likely to succeed. He's the boy voted most likely to take home to your parents. Randall is the typical type-A rule follower. He goes by the book. In the first episode when we meet Randall, he opens an email from a private investigator stating that they had found his father. Determined to pay his father a visit, he goes to his apartment and delivers a fantastic monologue about being a better man despite his father's absence. Yet, in an instant we see the deep yearning he has to be wanted and loved from his father. Soon we see an angry man invite this same man to his home while he battles cancer and has some mental issues.

In the beginning Randall appears to be put together. He has a beautiful family and all the money he could want. For someone who began with such a hard start in life, one would think he might have gone down a different life—a life of drugs and crime, bound by hurt and pain reeling from the sting of abandonment. But he has incredible compassion for people, including the man who left him on the steps of a firehouse with no contact and no explanation why. It's through Randall that we as an audience understand immense pain and ultimately forgiveness through that pain. We experience what it's like to be orphaned, losing his biological mother during childbirth and his biological father when he abandoned him. Then as a teenager Randall has lost the only father he ever knew, his rock, the one that literally carried him on his back as a small boy during karate class as he promised to rear him to be a man despite the cultural barriers of the color of their skins.

This is Us provides us with a unique glimpse into what it's like to be a black man living in a white world. As the seasons unfold, I can imagine how difficult the racial tensions must have been for him growing up. In the 80s when bullying was big but often unacknowledged, Randall faced his own share of mockery and scorn. From being called Webster (a reference to the main character in the 80s TV show) to his own brother not acknowledging him, he had not only his own questions of who he was going to become as a man but also the racial tensions of no one truly understanding who he was as a black boy.

Jack and Rebecca had much to face when it came to rearing children in the 80s and 90s. The world challenged Randall and tried to keep him down, but he rose above it. Yvette, the swimming pool parent whom Randall quickly befriends who quickly turns into a regular play date could only help so much. After being placed in a special school where he again was the minority, he not only had to face the realities of being physically different but also had to face being mentally different. In a tender scene where he goes to work with Jack, Jack asks him to do the math on one of his architectural plans. When Randall quickly finds the answer, the father asks him to do it again. He hesitates, and Jack questions him: "Why don't you want to tell me the answer?"

"Because they'll think I'm different," Randall says. "I don't want to be different. I want to be just like everyone else."

Even as adults, Randall is in a league of his own. Kate and Kevin are biological twins and share a bond Randall will never share with them. Married with two beautiful children, he has a life they wanted. Set apart not only by circumstances they could control but also by choices they have made, Kate and Kevin suffer the consequences of their mistakes. Randall, the rule follower has everything he has ever wanted within his grasp. Except, of course, for the love of his biological father.

Randall's desperation for his father's love is where he and the older brother in the prodigal son Bible story part ways. The eldest brother is angry with his father and remains that way, despite the father's attempt to invite him to the party. But Randall's anger is quickly replaced with compassion. He recognizes he can't stay angry at a man who's dying, and he needs to take full advantage of the time he has left with his father.

When we first meet Randall, he comes across as an angry rule follower, out to seek revenge from a father who abandoned him. But that perception is quickly abolished when he invites his father to his home to meet his grandkids and then stay with him so he can get the care and treatment he needs.

Jesus tells the crowd the parable of the prodigal son in the same context as the parable of the lost sheep and the lost coin. It's interesting that they're similar in context in the sense that the coin, sheep, and son are all lost and that Jesus will do anything to go after the lost in order for them to be found. But that's where the similarities end. Where the two sons' parable differs is that the sheep and the coin don't have the capacity to return on their own. Someone has to look for them. Conversely, a person has to decide on his/her own that they want to return to God rather than someone forcing them to be in that relationship. God will not force any of his children to have a relationship with him.   It's also interesting that, despite the fact that the father lovingly gives both sons their inheritance early, (even though to even ask for it early implies neither son cared at all about the father), the father doesn't chase after the son who has left. I can only imagine the pain and heartache the father felt to watch his son walk away.

Randall, Hospitality, and the Eldest Son

In the book <u>Righteous and Lost</u>, I speak about the eldest brother and his missed opportunity to display hospitality. The following is an excerpt from the book:

> The prodigal is much like the disciples in this passage in the sense is that he has nothing either. He has to rely on the generosity of his father. I can imagine his fear as he walked back home, having lived a wild life, wasting time, money and everything else. What would his father say? What

would his brother say? Should he even accept him, welcoming him back with open arms or turn him away and let him do the walk of shame back to the world that proved worthless?

What does the father do for the son: throws him a feast! The Prodigal Son parable is about hospitality, among other things. Around the dinner table is really the gateway from stranger to brother, and the fact that the eldest is hesitant to do so tells me he hesitates to have a strong bond with the prodigal. We know his father welcomed him back and the eldest doesn't, but the father invites the eldest into an opportunity to display hospitality and allow them to bond together as brothers." [1]

Instead of missing an opportunity, Randall shares all he has with his father, who really didn't deserve it. That's an example of Christian love we should all strive to imitate. Instead of closing off his heart to bitterness, he opens his heart to the possibility of love and approval from his father.

Fear and Randall

As much as Randall appears to have it all together, fear consumes him. Perhaps it's that he always had pressure to be number one because he felt like he head to earn his parents' love, so he didn't have to feel rejection of being abandoned again. He has struggled with panic attacks since

---

[1] Lazurek, Michelle. *Lost in Judgment: Discovering Hope for the Pharisee Within.* (Abilene: Leafwood Publishers. 2018.) p. 19.

he was a child, always feeling like he had to prove his worth to others. He puts undue pressure on himself at work, feeling replaced by co- worker Sanjay, who's equally as good at his job as Randall is his. Randall also feels overwhelmed as his father's health declines rapidly. When Randall's mother-in-law slips at home and breaks her hip, his wife has to go take care of her, leaving Randall to take care of things at home.

Although the tension has been mounting for a while, the moment arrives when extra issues send Randall over the edge. Besides his father's failing health, Randall takes in his brother Kevin when Kevin has nowhere to go and has make a mess of his life again, even though they haven't had a good relationship for a long time. In a later episode, we see Randall having a panic attack in the middle of his office, wracked with so much fear, it renders him incapacitated.

Dr. Archibald Hart in the book The Anxiety Cure writes, "Some life traumas, however, are known to increase one's risk for panic disorder. These traumas act to lower your 'threshold of tolerance' for stress by weakening your system's defenses. No doubt they also 'condition' you to experience exaggerated stress. When your ability to cope with stress drops, you experience increased stress. Stress creates more stress when it is not dealt with effectively."[2]

---

[2] Hart, Dr. Archibald. *The Anxiety Cure.* (Zondervan: Michigan:1999). P. 39.

Randall allows his stress defenses to drop with each life circumstance that he endured without accepting help. He doesn't want anyone to help take care of his father. He takes in Kevin even when his plate is already full, and he doesn't want to allow Sanjay to take his account at work. All of it together is allowing Randall's threshold for stress to increase. He can't even allow Kevin to beat him at running. He pushes himself to the limit, and it takes a toll on his body.

Huffington post wrote an article praising the show for its accurate portrayal of panic in a sufferer's life:

"The episode later reveals that Randall has anxiety, a common mental health disorder that affects an estimated 40 million Americans. Panic attacks, like Randall's, and panic disorder can often be coupled with anxiety. It's refreshing to not only see a panic attack portrayed on the small screen but a very accurate one at that. Randall's physical instability, disassociation, stress and tearfulness are all components of the issue — and it often springs up inconveniently and with no warning (like, say, before your brother's play). Fans of the show applauded the scene for being accurately executed and for offering those with mental illness encouragement, especially given the fact that misconceptions about mental health are still a massive societal issue: Research shows that negative stereotypes often stand in the way of people seeking medical treatment. When television shows, movies or celebrities tackle mental health publicly, experts say it helps to chip away at the deep rooted stigma that silences those with mental health issues."[3]

Breaking Free from Anxiety

Dr. Larry Crabb, renowned psychologist and Christian author, says,

"Imagine living under a powerful ruler who could prosper your life or blow you out of the water. Suppose he gave a series of commands that, if followed, would be rewarded with extravagant luxuries, but if disobeyed in any detail whatsoever, would result in agonizing torture. Further imagine that his laws included the requirements to never complain, to never irritably snap at anyone, to always put others' needs ahead of yours. Keep the law perfectly and enjoy unlimited blessings. Break one, just once, and you spend the rest of your life on the rack. And be aware, your ruler has eyes everywhere. No misstep will go unnoticed. If you managed to measure up to his standards for a time, you wouldn't rest in the blessings he gave. You'd be too worried about making a mistake. And when you'd fail, you would likely shout "unfair!' as you were hauled off to prison. 'You knew I couldn't perform to your standards. I never had a chance.' Life under the Law of Linearity would be unlivable.

---

[3] Holmes, Lindsay. "This Is Us' Totally Captured the Hard Truth About Panic Attacks." Huffington Post. http://bit.ly/2QzUG5l

But if someone delivered you from that arrangement (not because the law was unfair but because you weren't good enough to keep it) if someone found a way to let you live as a beloved son or daughter of the king with a royal position established not by performance but by relationship, you would probably be grateful. You one thought would be to get to know that person, to draw near to him. That story is true. It isn't a fairy tale. It happened. The Deliverer has come." [4]

By embracing the Savior's love and approval of us, we no longer have to be perfect. As compassionate and loving as Randall is, he still lives under this invisible law that as long as he's perfect, he is loved. But if he fails, even once, he will slip out of love and approval. Instead he wears a mask. That is, until Kevin finds him on the floor of his office in such a panicked state, he can't even get up. It was simply impossible for him to keep up the charade any longer.

Randall needs to be set free in the same way his brother and sister need to be set free. Randall needs to be released from comparison and perfectionism. Kevin needs to be set free from needing others' love and approval. Kate needs to be set free from needing a man's love to be made complete.

---

[4] Crabb, Dr. Larry. *The Pressure's Off.* (Colorado Springs, Waterbrook, 2002.) p. 31-32.

161

If Randall surrenders to God, he'll no longer need a job to complete his life. In the season one finale, we see a part of this surrender (although he doesn't surrender to God necessarily) as he walks in and quits his job after his boss and co-workers fail to support him after his father dies. His father has had a great impact in shaping who he is now.

Although they have only known each other for a few short months, William has shaped Randall in a positive way. He has learned to "crank up the radio, roll the window down," and enjoying the everyday moments of life instead of being so uptight about everything.

We would do well to do the same.

For the past 16 years I have put everything and
everyone ahead of myself, you and the kids, and I
just knew if I were ever to tell you about this
whole Ben thing that you would spin out, and I
needed to have something for myself without you
getting in the way.

Rebecca

Chapter Thirteen
Rebecca and the Modern-Day Rebekah

Rebecca, one of the most complicated characters, is one whom most people love or hate. Some people don't like her because she presents the opposite of Jack, at times selfish and unappreciative of Jack's sacrifices (for example, forgetting his birthday) and for putting Jack in such an awkward position with wanting to go on tour for her singing career with an ex-boyfriend from her youth. But there's a certain charm to Rebecca that fans cannot ignore such as her beautiful monologue to her children in the womb just before she goes into labor and her attempt at a seductive dance to make Jack happy on his birthday even when she is almost full term in her pregnancy and not feeling (or looking) her best. As a mother, she has made her share of sacrifices, too. Rebecca made it clear she didn't want to have children, except a tryst with Jack in the bar bathroom after the Steelers game results in conceiving Kevin and Kate.

From the first look of Rebecca as an older woman, a proud grandma to Randall's children, happy wife to Miguel, and once love of Jack's life, she appears on the surface as content with life, proud of her achievements and ready to see where the rest of her life takes her. But on the inside, she harbors a secret.

Soon after Randall meets and invites his father to live with him, we learn that Rebecca and William have met before. In fact, they are more than mere acquaintances. Rebecca tracked William down after spotting him outside the hospital after they agreed to take Randall home shortly after his birth. She found him at his home and made him promise to never see Randall again. No contact, no letters, no phone calls. Threatened by the potential danger of William getting Randall back, she ensures William never contacts him, but not before William gives her a book of his favorite poems by his favorite poet, Dudley Randall, prompting Rebecca to change his name to Randall, setting him apart from his siblings.

Although Rebecca appeared to make a sweet first connection with William years ago, she confessed she had trouble bonding with her non-biological son named Kyle. She denied William's earnest, sheepish request to check in on his son from time to time, insisting that she needed to establish her (and Jack's) boundaries as the parents, perhaps worried that the child would, ultimately, be taken from her. But she did take William's advice and change Kyle's name to something non-K. The child was his own person, explained William, thus, suggesting the name "Randall" after the poet Dudley Randall, whose book *Counterpoem* William gives her as a gift. "Maybe you'll see fit to give it to him someday," William said hopefully, and *Counterpoem* did become a staple of Randall's bookshelf.

Dan Fogelman, the producer, commented on this episode: "They were into it. It was the first thing we did when Mandy was [playing the older version of Rebecca]. When older Rebecca goes and dresses him down, I wanted to make sure that all felt right, and you could hear a pin drop with our crew. Nobody was talking. You were afraid to breathe on the set. You knew there was something here, and you almost feel like these characters were real, so it was very intense. We did two takes, and [directors John Requa and Glenn Ficarra] knew we had it."[1]

But Rebecca's fear of loss goes much deeper than a fear of losing her son. In the episode when Kevin, Kate, and Randall go up to visit the cabin they used to go to every year, there is a telling scene where Randall gets a glimpse of Rebecca's life. After learning Rebecca's secret that she knew Randall's father his whole life and kept him a secret from him, he flashes back to when they were kids happily playing games and eating popcorn. After hallucinating that his father is talking to him, he watches as Rebecca happily plays homemaker during the day, yet frantically closes all doors and windows, locking them to keep the bad things out.

While we're still unsure why this is the case, we do know that Rebecca's overprotection of Randall has more to do with her childhood issues then Randall's. This is when the audience sympathizes with Rebecca.

---

[1] Snierson, Dan. "This Is Us Creator Dan Fogleman Breaks Down Rebecca's Secret." Entertainment. http://bit.ly/2pzZf43

As a mother, I understand Rebecca's desire to keep her kids close to her. Having suffered the loss of a child, I can imagine she never wants to experience the pain of losing another child. Although some critics argue this was a selfish move by not telling Randall about his father. However, her motives although slightly selfish are, in essence, noble.

Rebecca parallels so distinctly with the Rebekah of the Old Testament:

> Now Rebekah was listening as Isaac spoke to his son Esau. When Esau left for the open country to hunt game and bring it back, Rebekah said to her son Jacob, "Look, I overheard your father say to your brother Esau, 'Bring me some game and prepare me some tasty food to eat, so that I may give you my blessing in the presence of the Lord before I die.' Now, my son, listen carefully and do what I tell you: Go out to the flock and bring me two choice young goats, so I can prepare some tasty food for your father, just the way he likes it. Then take it to your father to eat, so that he may give you his blessing before he dies." Jacob said to Rebekah his mother, "But my brother Esau is a hairy man while I have smooth skin. What if my father touches me? I would appear to be tricking him and would bring down a curse on myself rather than a blessing." His mother said to him, "My son, let the curse fall on me. Just do what I say; go and get them for me." So he went and got them and brought

them to his mother, and she prepared some tasty food, just the way his father liked it. Then Rebekah took the best clothes of Esau her older son, which she had in the house, and put them on her younger son Jacob. She also covered his hands and the smooth part of his neck with the goatskins. Then she handed to her son Jacob the tasty food and the bread she had made (Genesis 27:5-17).

Rebecca is the antithesis to Jack. Jack is the lovable, nice guy. Raised in a dysfunctional home, he's the war veteran who fixes his elderly neighbor's car and then sells that car to buy a house for Rebecca. He takes a job and sacrifices his dreams to provide for his family.

Rebecca, on the other hand, appears as though she only thinks about herself: getting up in the middle of a blind date so she could sing at an open mic night; telling Jack she feels unfulfilled and has no life as a mother and wife because her singing career never took off. In comparison to Jack, she is a bit self-absorbed.

As I have watched the show I can agree with the notion that she is, indeed, selfish. At least, that's how she's portrayed. On Instagram, actress Mandy Moore, who plays Rebecca, even shared her real life parents' text to her after the season finale. They told her, "Rebecca was mean for the fight she had with Jack!"

But as a mother, I have had those same longings, said those same things, and felt terrible after I said them. Rebecca encapsulates many mothers' and wives' feelings about being unfulfilled in a career. When I became a writer, it filled the hole I was lacking in my soul. It was what I was meant to do, although I hadn't pursued it on my own. When I began writing, I realized I was able to use gifts and talents I never knew I possessed. I felt blessed to be able to use my gifts to spread the Gospel in ways I felt I wasn't doing before working in other jobs.

From a Christian standpoint, we should on some level understand what Rebecca is going through. When we don't discover and utilize the spiritual gifts we've been given, we grow complacent. We sit in our same pew week after week sometimes wasting the opportunities God has given us. First Corinthians 12: 12-14; 28-31 speak to this idea:

> Just as a body, though one, has many parts, but all its many parts form one body, so it is with Christ. For we were all baptized by one Spirit so as to form one body—whether Jews or Gentiles, slave or free—and we were all given the one Spirit to drink. Even so the body is not made up of one part but of many. Now you are the body of Christ, and each one of you is a part of it. And God has placed in the church first of all apostles, second prophets, third teachers, then miracles, then gifts of healing, of helping, of guidance, and of different kinds of tongues. Are all apostles? Are all prophets? Are all teachers? Do all work miracles? Do all have gifts of healing? Do all speak in tongues? Do all interpret? Now eagerly desire the greater gifts.

Just like the church should desire to want to be used in a powerful way, this is what Rebecca wants too. She just wants to be used to make a difference in others' lives.

Her plea is the cry of everyone's heart. To know and be known. From Rebecca and Jack's fight, we see she's not feeling like she's being used in that way, and it's leaving her feeling stuck.

Jack and Rebecca's Meeting Changes Their Lives

I want you to swear by the LORD, the God of heaven and the God of earth, that you will not get a wife for my son from the daughters of the Canaanites, among whom I am living, but will go to my country and my own relatives and get a wife for my son Isaac." Then he prayed, "LORD, God of my master Abraham, make me successful today, and show kindness to my master Abraham. See, I am standing beside this spring, and the daughters of the townspeople are coming out to draw water. May it be that when I say to a young woman, 'Please let down your jar that I may have a drink,' and she says, 'Drink, and I'll water your camels too'—let her be the one you have chosen for your servant Isaac. By this I will know that you have shown kindness to my master." Before he had finished praying, Rebekah came out with her jar on her shoulder. She was the daughter of Bethuel son of Milkah, who was the wife of Abraham's brother Nahor. The woman was very beautiful, a virgin; no man had ever slept with her. She went down to the spring, filled her jar and came up again" (Genesis 24:3, 12-16).

This passage from Genesis 24 is similar to the way Jack meets Rebecca. Jack, feeling down about life and feeling like he needs to change himself to be "bad" so he can be a winner in life, goes to a local bar to steal the money he lost in a poker game. But before he approaches the register, he hears the most beautiful voice ever, which belongs to Rebecca. They meet after her set, and the rest is history.

It appears to be a divine appointment in more ways than one. Not only did Jack and Rebecca have blind dates scheduled with other people, but Rebecca saves Jack from making a terrible mistake that might have ruined his life. In the same way that Isaac prayed to find the right woman to take as a wife, Jack needed Rebecca in his life to save him physically and spiritually. Their meeting sends them on a trajectory of a life they could have only had with each other.

Enjoying more love than most couples do and becoming parents to three children, they also had to go through tough times together as well. Losing a child is possibly one of the most devastating experiences ever; yet, they had each other to lean on. In another chance encounter, they're able to save Randall's life by adopting him into their family and making them their own.

172

But as much as her presence is a saving grace to Jack's less-than-stellar upbringing, her life is equally as unstable. By the end of season one, out of all of the characters in this show, we know the least about Rebecca's life. We have only received a couple brief glimpses of her past, and the few we have received tell us there are some deep wounds and pain with which Rebecca deals. The only flashback we have of Rebecca is at the beginning of the episode "The Game Plan."

The episode begins with Rebecca and her sister as young girls watching a Steelers game with their dad. Her mother is running around the house, desperate to wait on her father and get him his lunch. As she sets a sandwich and chips down in front of him, he doesn't repay her with a kiss on the cheek or even a "thank you" her way. Instead, he glares at her, and with one word demonstrates he has little respect for her.

"Beer?' he grumbles.

The mother runs to the fridge, grabs the beer, opens it for him, and sets it down before him on the tray. She then quickly says, "Girls, you're going to have to play somewhere else. Your father is watching the game."

From the beginning of her life, she's been cast aside because she wasn't a guy. Even when she's yelling at the television in the following scene after she has asked Jack to help her understand football, she's the only female interested in the game at the bar. During that time, females were cast aside. They're expected to stay at home, take care of the kids, leave the husband to his own life, and be content in their role to cook up the bacon their husbands bring home. However, it's obvious that's not the type of life she wants (which may be part of the reason why she doesn't want children.)

By the season finale, we realize she has been cast aside her entire life. This is even evident in her conversation with her friends as a young woman. Excited to tell her friends about how well things are going and her leap to send a demo tape to a friend's contact at a recording company, Rebecca bucks at current trends.

Her friends think otherwise. "We think things are going great for you. You have a great singing voice, and we think you can make it. But what if you don't make it? I mean, do you think it may be time to diversify?" Even her friends don't really believe she should have a career and forsake marriage and children. It was what the culture at that tie dictated for women, and her friends were quick to convince her she might miss out on life if she doesn't pursue it the conventional way.

I'm not sure much has changed since then. Even as much as we have progressed from archaic ideals of yesteryear, society still buys into the lie that the best place for a woman is in the home. And she should always be smiling while she's there.

Rebecca's lack of happiness will not be solved relaxing at a spa. Rebecca is an intelligent, strong, talented woman who just wants to be given the same opportunity to use her gifts to make a mark on the world. No manicure or hot stone massage is going to fulfill that in the same way as using her talent for song. Women who have said this to themselves are silently cheering, even if audiences are initially jeering at Rebecca's character.

Rebecca has had to make sacrifices, too, but society doesn't recognize that as readily because as a woman that is her "role." We revere Jack for his sacrifices yet completely ignore Rebecca for hers. Jack's goading her to "say it, tell me we are not enough for you" is really the turning point in Rebecca's life and their marriage. Neither of them could not take back what they had said.

Jack is insecure about Rebecca admitting that she's not happy in the marriage and wants more out of life than a marriage and children. This leads to their unofficial separation although in later seasons this may play a role in their disillusion of their relationship well before he ever dies.

A Deep Dark Secret

As Randall grapples with Rebecca's decision to keep his father's identity from him, he gets a glimpse into his mother's life and a possible explanation as to why she is the way she is. Jack reveals to Randall at that fateful scene at the cabin that Rebecca had "her own things she had to deal with."

The scene finds Rebecca late at night running around the house, closing windows, and triple-checking locks on the doors after Jack and the kids have gone to bed. This may not be out of place at their home in Pittsburgh but in a secluded cabin? This tells us there are secrets that lie well below the surface from her childhood that cause her to act such a protective way with Randall.

As seasons unfold, I believe we'll gain more insight as to why her father dismissed her throughout her life and why she's not happy to go over to her mother's house on Thanksgiving.

We catch a glimpse of Rebecca's inadequacy as a mother as she deals with some post-partum depression and general feeling of being overwhelmed after they bring the triplets home. Rebecca again demonstrates that not every woman was born with the instincts to rear a child. This hesitancy that we see is possibly a clue that there may be more to Rebecca's story than we've been told at this point.

This Is Us gives a voice for what many women have felt throughout the generations. While they enjoy caring for their families, they want to do things that stretch their minds and utilize their abilities. In the same way we Christians feel about our role within the church body, Rebecca feels that way about her life. Women should not feel embarrassed or ashamed about wanting to pursue a career. If there's one theme *This Is Us* communicates it's that women can be strong yet care for their families all while pursuing their dreams.

Thus, we see another reason to be grateful for a show that teaches women to reach for the stars.

Jack:
So I'm gonna need everyone in this room to believe that only good things are going to happen today. Actually, I need you to know it. Do you know it, baby?

Rebecca:
I love you baby. Yeah, I know it.

Jack:
Do you know it, doc?

Chapter Fourteen
Jack and the Modern-Day King David

"They took the wrong son!" Johnny Cash's father shouts at him after an accident on the family farm takes his older brother's life. In the movie *Walk the Line,* Joaquin Phoenix portrays Johnny Cash and his life from a young boy who survives his father's constant physical and emotional abuse as well as his rise to stardom. From door-to-door vacuum salesman to singing Gospel songs with his band, Cash takes a chance and auditions for a local producer who asks him to sing a song that is "believable." He then sings a song he had been toying with now known as "Folsom Prison Blues." Although he's humble and is a loving husband who dotes on his two children, his inner demons from his childhood revisit him as an adult. To believe he's not good enough slowly takes its toll, and he succumbs to numb his loneliness with alcohol. Soon the alcohol controls everything, and he can no longer perform without alcohol. This model of the music world, this up-and-coming star who appears like he has everything in the world has demons he can't control.

Jack can understand this as he comes from a similar situation. In one of the few scenes we have of Jack's family when he goes to ask his father for money, his father makes him repeat the mantra, "Yeah, Dad, I'm never going to be anything in life."

As a married man, Jack wants to do the right thing for Rebecca and his children. He takes a desk job instead of pursuing his dream to build his own business, he sells his favorite car (a 1967 Chevelle Super Sport) to get enough money to stay in their apartment, and he puts a down payment on a house so he can make his wife happy.

Jack, by television standards, is a modern-day hero. A humble mechanic who served in Vietnam, he plays it off when his neighbor, Mrs. Peabody asks him, "Why are you so nice? Most of those boys who come back from there have lost their minds."

In fact, I often see T-shirts that don the phrase, "I have a Jack," implying that the person wearing the shirt has a wonderful, sacrificial mate whom they love. From the first episode we're tempted to put Jack on a pedestal, one of the best examples of a husband TV has seen since the 1980s.

One of the many factors that gives *This Is Us* its appeal is it's one of the first television shoes that portrays a male character as a positive role model. His kids adore him, his wife often refers to him as "the love of her life," and he's respected in his job. Not since the days of Dick Van Dyke, *Father Knows Best*, and *The Donna Reed Show* have men been portrayed as strong, competent figures on television. Since the late 80s when Al Bundy came on the scene, TV morphed from men being the head of the house who took care of their families and took pride in their work to a lousy salesman who hated his wife and spends most of his life fitting ugly shoes for even uglier women. That trend continues in some of the much beloved comedies that graced our sets throughout the 90s and into the new Millennium.

This Is Us, however, raises the bar for television. Jack is now the example of what a good family looks like. He's the knight that women wish would come in and rescue them from their ordinary lives. After the first three episodes, we wonder if Jack has any negative qualities whatsoever. He's never tired when he gets home from work, he's always there to encourage and help his wife out when needed, and the Big three song. He sings with his kids is adorable! But it isn't long before we find there is a chink in the knight's armor.

A Chink in the Armor

In the season one finale, Jack and his friend are sitting outside his home just days before he meets Rebecca for the first time. He's just gone to a poker game that his friend Darryl's cousin runs. There he wins a significant amount of money so he can get his own place. But the owners beat him up outside and take the money, threatening to kill him if they ever see Jack or Darryl there again.

At that moment, Jack's tired of being the good guy. He has sacrificed everything for everyone and has not received much in return. He talks to Darryl about his father and says,

"You know, I watched him over the years, my father, and whenever he had the choice between doing the right thing and doing the wrong thing he always broke to the wrong way, like clockwork, wrong, wrong, wrong, every single time. For me, you know I tried to go the other way. Be respectful to women, do my part in 'Nam, be a good man, and look where it's gotten me. When am I going to get my break, Darryl? When? The punks, they make this too hard, man, just too damn hard. Next week we're going back to that bar and we're going to win our money back, and I'm going to take the life that I was supposed to have instead of it waiting to come find me." Jack thinks it's finally time to be bad, to take from the world what he feels it has for him.

For a moment we see Jack has a sinful side. He turns from a giving and kind servant to a selfish, greedy thief. Things are turned around however, when he hears the most beautiful voice come from the most beautiful woman he's ever seen. It's here he meets Rebecca, and his life is never the same. He says it's "his big break."

Some could argue the moment he meets Rebecca is the best thing that's ever happened to him, with which Jack would agree; yet, others would say it's the worst.

Despite their beautiful children, the feeling that life has dealt them a bad hand will always stay with them. The argument is a trigger for both of their deep-seated wounds and pain to come forward.

Rebecca says, "You're not a drunk, Jack, you're not. You drank too much for one year seven years ago, and then you stopped cold turkey but I do find it convenient that this sudden alcoholism of yours has suddenly rematerialized at the exact moment that I have something finally happening for myself." Rebecca is referring to Jack's first bout with drinking. From early in the season we know that Jack has a problem with alcohol. After coming home from the bar a bit tipsy in episode three, Rebecca confronts him to set the record straight. "The drinking has to stop, Jack. You have to reign it in, baby, because I won't have it in my house."

He vows to become "the man she deserves," only to have his demons haunt him several more times. In episode eighteen titled, "Moonshadow," we see just how much alcoholism has taken over his life. As he drives two hours to see Rebecca on tour, the camera closes in on the backseat that has nine empty beer cans quickly joined by the one Jack finishes and throws in the back.

"You're not just my great love story, Rebecca, you were my big break," he told her before nodding to the wedding vows that Rebecca read to him many years before. "And our love story, I know it may not feel like it right now, but baby... I promise you, it's just getting started." One parallel that "Moonshadow" teaches us about Jack is his tendency to turn from good guy to bad boy in a short period of time. That action on his part is what makes him a flawed character. Rebecca appears to be Jack's savior—not only saving him from making a potentially life-altering mistake of stealing the money from the bar's open till but also canceling her tour to get him to stop punching her ex-boyfriend.

Apparently, the group at that fateful night of poker taught him a lesson he takes with him until later on in life—to get what you want, you have to use whatever means necessary, even if it means violence or abuse.

Apparently, Jack and King David in the Bible had more in common than we thought.

Jack's Past is a Part of His Present

Jack's the son of an abusive drunk. He's a nice guy and willing to fix anything for anyone. He keeps the peace with his father, who degrades him from the minute he walks through the door of his home until he leaves, but secretly Jack's desperate to get himself and his mom out of that house. With big plans to start his own company, even before meeting Rebecca, he constantly puts his own needs aside for the wellbeing of others. But his jealousy and inner rage can only hold off for so long. After learning Rebecca has had a relationship with one of the band members, she is going on tour with, Jack's inner demons are too tempting to resist. In a drunken rage, he punches the band member and embarrasses Rebecca. Having to drive him home, she quits the band, causing her own resentment of not being able to pursue her dreams. In the season finale, Rebecca and Jack have one of their biggest fights, both showing their true colors. Jack wants to be enough for Rebecca, and Rebecca wants to pursue something for herself so that she can be fulfilled in her career.

This is a big turning point in Jack and Rebecca's relationship. No matter how much they try to smooth things over, it can never go back to the way things were. No longer can they live in their delusions that they are happy in their marriage. As much as they love each other, love is not enough. Jack's alcoholism is too difficult to control and Rebecca's constant yearning for something more will always take precedence over the sacrifices they have made, and those sacrifices will become nothing more than a gateway to martyrdom as each thinks he/she owes the other one something because life hasn't gone the way they planned. Jack can't let Rebecca go for fear of losing her, and Rebecca wants to be free and soar; yet, everyone in her life holds her back from being the person she is meant to be.

During the big fight scene in the season one finale, Jack quickly reveals why he is so jealous of Rebecca's career: "Say it. Say we are enough." We understand that although Jack has willingly sacrificed himself to put his wife and family's needs first, we know there is a secret jealousy that Jack never got to achieve his dream career. The fact he learns Rebecca is going on tour with a band that includes her ex-boyfriend is just a cover for the inner envy that has been kept at bay for so long.

The great irony of Jack is that he wants Rebecca to be fulfilled only by him and their children. However, he is not fulfilled only by them, as evidenced by his first battle with alcohol when the kids were ten years old.

Rebecca puts an end to his drinking with an ultimatum that either he quit drinking or he can't stay at the house. Jack vows to end it and keeps his word until years later. But the big question many fans ask is, "Why did he need to start drinking in the first place?" He had everything he could have ever wanted: a wife that adored him, three great kids, and a beautiful home. Yet, there is a hole in his heart that needs to be filled. The season one finale points to another possible element to the destruction of Jack and Rebecca's marriage: gambling.

Jack and his friend participate in a poker game that ends up earning Jack a bunch of money. Eager to cash out, Jack and his friend exit, only to be surprised by the members of the game who brutally attack him in the parking lot. It remains to be seen if gambling will be another vice that gets in the way of Jack and his great life, but it's enough for audiences to know he has more than one dragon to slay.

In an article from bustle.com, Sabienna Bowman says:

"As amazing as he is as a father and husband, Jack has his demons. He struggles with drinking issues and jealousy, and no matter how hard he tries, he never completely escapes the money troubles that have plagued him all his life. With three kids about to head off to college and a marriage he's helplessly trying to hold together, Jack could easily fall back into gambling.... If he enters a self-destructive period in his life again, he might find himself at

186

another poker table, this time in hopes of scoring enough money to follow his dreams of starting his own business *and* keep his family stable and happy. Remember, Rebecca isn't the only one who put her dreams on hold for the sake of the children. Jack wanted to be a small business owner, but it wasn't possible when he had three children to support. There is nothing he wouldn't sacrifice for his kids, but in the process, Jack has created a life where he is overworked, insecure, and frustrated by all the dreams he gave up on."[2]

Sound familiar? King David had everything he could have ever wanted. A beautiful wife and the respect of the people around him when he assumed his position as king, even though he wasn't the first choice for king.

Under God's direction, Samuel was to select the new king of Israel. Although everyone was looking for a rugged and popular member of Jesse's sons, God knew the hearts of everyone. He knew David had a heart for God, and appointed him as king, despite everyone's surprise:

Then Jesse had Shammah come to Samuel. "The LORD has not chosen this one either," Samuel said. So Jesse brought seven more of his sons to Samuel, but Samuel told Jesse, "The LORD has not chosen any of these. Are these all the sons you have?"

---

[2] Bowman, Sabienna. "The 'This Is Us' Finale May Have Foreshadowed Jack's Death, If You Belive This Erie Theory." Bustle. http://bit.ly/2IDv3xz

"There's still the youngest one," Jesse answered. "He's tending the sheep."

Samuel told Jesse, "Send someone to get him. We won't continue until he gets here" (1 Samuel 16:9-11). So David was anointed as God's chosen one. Everyone doubted the choice, that is, until David took on Goliath when no one else would. When he defeated him despite his youth and lack of resources, he quickly earned the people's respect, much to Samuel's dismay.

David had it all. Just like Jack saw Rebecca singing and it was love at first sight, he chose his wife to be the love of her life. And things were going great for a while, until David lays eyes on Bathsheba:

> "Now, when evening came, David got up from his bed and walked around on the roof of the royal palace. From the roof he saw a woman bathing, and she was very pretty. David sent someone to ask about the woman. The man said, 'She's Bathsheba, daughter of Eliam and wife of Uriah the Hittite'" (2 Samuel 11).

Becoming the king of Israel is the changing moment for David. Slowly his ego is built up from his conquests. Slowly the power and the prestige get the best of him, and soon his marriage is not enough either. He's tempted by lust and beauty, paired with the ease of having anything he wants, and the combination sets him on a destructive path. The rest of David's story is what Christians focus on: his indiscretion with Bathsheba, his murder attempt on her husband to cover it up, and the subsequent pregnancy, birth, and death of their son strips David of the very things that set him on that path in the first place. Once David lays eyes on Bathsheba, his whole life changes. In the same way, as soon as Jack takes that first drink after his huge fight with Rebecca after promising her to not drink again, everything changes. Soon he can no longer survive without drinking to the point of excess. David's lust for women leads to his downfall, and Jack's lust for alcohol leads to his downfall too.

King David knew something about this in his life. A lowly shepherd tending sheep out in the field wasn't even being considered for the role of cupbearer to the king. Yet, God, who sees all, had groomed David for this position:

> When they arrived, Samuel saw Eliab and thought, "Surely the LORD's anointed stands here before the LORD." But the LORD said to Samuel, "Do not consider his appearance or his height, for I have rejected him. The LORD does not look at the things people look at. People look at the outward appearance, but the LORD looks at the heart."

> Then Jesse called Abinadab and had him pass in front of Samuel. But Samuel said, "The LORD has not chosen this one either." Jesse then had Shammah pass by, but Samuel said, "Nor has the LORD chosen this one." Jesse had seven of his sons pass before Samuel, but Samuel said to him, "The LORD has not chosen these." So he asked Jesse, "Are these all the sons you have?"

"There is still the youngest," Jesse answered. "He is tending the sheep." Samuel said, "Send for him; we will not sit down until he arrives." So he sent for him and had him brought in. He was glowing with health and had a fine appearance and handsome features. Then the LORD said, "Rise and anoint him; this is the one. So Samuel took the horn of oil and anointed him in the presence of his brothers, and from that day on the Spirit of the LORD came powerfully upon David. Samuel then went to Ramah." (1 Samuel 16:7).

A seeming nobody, David had been overlooked by people, too. Plucked from the fields of his humble beginnings, he was chosen to play the lyre for Saul. But when David kills Goliath and eventually is chosen to be king, Saul's love for David quickly turns into hate:

Saul was afraid of David, because the LORD was with David but had departed from Saul. So he sent David away from him and gave him command over a thousand men, and David led the troops in their campaigns. In everything he did he had great success, because the LORD was with him. When Saul saw how successful he was, he was afraid of him. But all Israel and Judah loved David, because he led them in their campaigns." (1 Samuel 18: 12-16.)

Much like David became humble after the death of his son, Jack returns to his original humble attitude when he gives a tear-jerking monologue to Rebecca about their relationship: "You asked me to tell you what I love about

190

you, so I'm going to start with the obvious. I love the mother that you are. I love that you are still the most beautiful woman in any room and that you laugh with your entire face. I love that you dance funny, and I love that you are still the same woman that after all those years ago ran out of a blind date because you just had to sing. You are not just my great love story, Rebecca, you are our love story. And our love story, even though it may not feel like it right now, I promise you, is just getting started." A humble confession from a humble man who is in love with his wife and wants to make amends for all the wrongs he has committed in his life.

David wanted to make amends too:

> Then David said to Nathan, "I have sinned against the LORD." Nathan answered, "The LORD has taken away your sin. You will not die. But what you did caused the LORD's enemies to lose all respect for him. For this reason the son who was born to you will die." Then Nathan went home. And the LORD caused the son of David and Bathsheba, Uriah's widow, to be very sick. David prayed to God for the baby. David fasted and went into his house and stayed there, lying on the ground all night. The elders of David's family came to him and tried to pull him up from the ground, but he refused to get up or to eat food with them (2 Samuel 12:13-15).

This is a quick fall from the pedestal on which David once stood. Jack falls from grace quickly too, despite the many chances Rebecca has given him over the years.

David's decisions end up destroying the happiness he had just a short time ago.

We are glad Jack's destructive choices haven't destroyed the happy family he has too.

You see, for days, I've been plagued by the question: How do I honor my father's legacy? Then I realized, I honor his legacy by taking what I learned from the way he lived his life and use it to shape the way I go on living mine. So here it is, Tyler. I quit.

Randall

Chapter Fifteen
William and the Modern-Day Prodigal Son

"Roll your window down. Crank up the music. Take me to meet your father," a surprisingly peaceful William says to an uptight Randall after he doesn't want to take William to see where some of Jack's ashes are scattered. A half day out of the way seems too much to Randall when they have to get to Memphis; yet, the timing is perfect for William, who uses it as an opportunity to make peace with the man who reared his son as well as making peace with himself.

"Thank you," William says to Jack, "for doing what I couldn't do, for raising him to be the man he is. I'm sorry I didn't get a chance to meet you, brother. I would have liked to have heard that laugh. I would have liked to have met my son's father." A humbling speech, free of pretense or pride, laced with gratitude. Gratitude that the Lord provided Randall with a good man who would carry Randall on his back (literally) if that meant he could rear him in the ways he should go.

In the episode titled, "Memphis," we get a glimpse into William's life. A truly impoverished man, having never had a father growing up (he died serving his country), I can imagine the deprivations in his soul, of not feeling like he could measure up to his father's legacy. War heroes are hard to shadow, and in William's case, he probably felt like he had dishonored his family name by getting addicted to drugs, falling in love with a woman and giving birth to a baby out of wedlock, only to place the infant on a doorstep just a few days later.

By the end of the episode, it alludes to the fact that William knew he wasn't going to be going home with Randall, which is why he wrote a note to Randall's wife and spoke to his grandchildren before he left that day. It's a day to make peace, peace with the family he let down when he promised his cousin he would write more music but let him down, a chance to make peace with Jack, the father who raised William, as well as a chance to make peace with Randall, a son who freely offered him forgiveness even when William felt he didn't deserve it. Ironically, it's a peace that Randall, the good son, the one that followed all the rules, has trouble receiving.

Putting so much pressure on himself even since he was a child, Randall suffers from anxiety attacks, placing him in an almost incomprehensible state. The person who "seems to have it all together" as William puts it, planned the trip to Memphis as an attempt to give him that peace he has never had for himself. If there's one thing William teaches his son, it's teaching him to lie back, relax, and get the most out of every day because tomorrow is never promised.

William has something very much in common with the prodigal son. The Bible story tells of two sons: one squanders, one saves, both are lost. In a striking parallel, watching Randall and William's relationship play out is like watching the parable play out in real life. Randall is the stern older brother, the rule father, astonished at how easy he can take life. William, on the other hand, is the prodigal, an impoverished man, seeking to make peace with the mistakes he has made in the past and seeking forgiveness from the son rather than a father.

One of the most gripping scenes is of William visiting the home in which he grew up with his single mother, with whom he lived until she died. When he enters the house he goes to the fireplace where he extracts a loose brick that uncovers a couple of toys and three quarters he had stashed away when he was a kid. This scene reveals William for who he really is: a truly poor man. Now he gets a chance to revisit that poverty, revel in all he has received since then, yet reflect on how much he had lost, too.

Life has a way of reminding us how much we've lost yet still have gained with God's mighty hand of provision. Although William has nothing of value to give to Randall, no fortune, no promises of making a name in the world, we see William writing a song that his cousin had sung many years ago. Unfortunately, the band never fully launches its career due to William falling in love with Randall's biological mother and after his own mother's passing becoming addicted to drugs because of a girlfriend's influence.

Haunted by this realization, William visits the cousin on this fateful trip in an attempt to make peace, but to no avail. A real life portrayal of the older and younger brother as well, the prodigal doesn't even make an attempt to reconcile with his older brother but only accepts the grace and hospitality of his father. But why?

Perhaps it's because there's no true fellowship with others until we can accept the our father's love and forgiveness for our transgressions, but the parable doesn't tell us this, it only hints at it. Everything William owns that is of any value is in that car with him: his oxygen tank, his pocket of trinkets from his childhood home, and a son who openly extends forgiveness after true repentance.
The Prodigal Son parable states:

> Jesus continued: "There was a man who had two sons. The younger one said to his father, 'Father, give me my share of the estate.'" So he divided his property between them. Not long after that, the younger son got together all he had, set off for a distant country and there squandered his wealth in wild living. After he had spent everything, there was a severe famine in that whole country, and he began to be in need. So he went and hired himself out to a citizen of that country, who sent him to his fields to feed pigs. [16] He longed to fill his stomach with the pods that the pigs were eating, but no one gave him anything. "When he came to his senses, he said, 'How many of my father's hired servants have food to spare, and here I am starving to death! I will set out and go back to my father and say to him: Father, I have sinned against heaven and against you. I am no longer worthy to be called your son; make me like one of your hired servants.' So he got up and went to his father. But while he was

still a long way off, his father saw him and was filled with compassion for him; he ran to his son, threw his arms around him and kissed him." The son said to him, 'Father, I have sinned against heaven and against you. I am no longer worthy to be called your son.'" (Luke 15:11-32.)

When William first arrives at his childhood home, doesn't go in. "I can't stop looking at the door. There used to be two doors, and now one is bricked up. Isn't that a strange thing to focus on? All these years and it's a door that's hanging me up." William seizes the opportunity to break through the door, to walk through the cobwebs of his soul, and stop getting hung up on the doors that were keeping him from letting go.

If only we could all walk through the bricked-up parts of our soul and break free from the restrictions that keep us from walking free in Christ. The prodigal son did it; William did it. Perhaps it's time for us to do it too.

But there's a price to pay for our freedom. With the prodigal son, in order for him to fully accept the father's love, he had to reign in his wild heart. His desire to go out and squander all of his money comes from a heart of rebellion wracked with pain.

To ease his pain instead of running to Christ, William ran to whatever else would ease his aching soul: alcohol and sex. Instead of achieving intimacy with God, he achieved intimacy with friends (who were more than willing to waste his money until he had none.)

What's important to note is that the father in the parable never chases after the son. He never pleads with him saying, "Son, it's okay. We'll work it out. Don't worry about it." There are always consequences to sin.

Our Heavenly Father knows that. He doesn't want a relationship with someone who doesn't want one with Him. He doesn't want a person going through the motions of the faith, sending up superficial prayers; He wants our hearts. He wants us to desire a relationship with Him. The earthly father knew that the prodigal son had to repent before he could reconcile. The son had to be at the lowest point in his life before he could see what he had truly lost.

Randall meets his father at that exact moment, too. William is dying. In the throes of pain and stage four cancer, he's at his lowest point. He's faced with the consequences of his sin, too. God allows him the chance to make amends with the people whom he has wronged and make peace with the consequences of his choices. When his mother passes, William then turns to drugs to cope. He didn't start out that way, but eventually the pain of life and the desire for love and to fulfill the need for intimacy are too much to handle, so he does drugs. Soon, the way to cope with situations results from outside sources that control him rather than him controlling those situations. In order for him to soothe the cry of his heart to love and be loved, he turns to alternate ways to fulfill his yearnings, including exploring sexuality with men.

His relationship with Jessie is revealed on Christmas Eve, and some would argue comes completely out of the blue. But isn't that just another way to fill the gaping hole inside his heart? Don't we all look for love in other ways to cope with the separation we have from God since the fall of man?

Since TV is a reflection of our culture, *This is Us* allows William's character to explore the culture and society the same way the world does. Sexuality and gender are being redefined all the time. No longer are male and female the only two choices in gender, nor is straight or gay the only choices in expressing sexuality.

In an article in Time magazine titled, "Beyond He or She," author Katy Steinmetz states: "Many young people have, from a very early age, known people who are out. GLAAD's survey found that Millennials were, for example, about twice as likely as boomers to have someone in their circles who identifies as bisexual, a sexual, queer or questioning. " [1]

Similarly, Diane Sawyer recently interviewed Kaitlyn Jenner two years after having the final surgery to transition to a woman. Caitlyn, a seemingly more confident person as a woman, talked openly about both the positive and negative consequences of her transition. Although she said she had no regrets, she did want to use her celebrity status to initiate and further the conversation about

---

[1] Steinmetz, Katy. "Beyond He or She: How a New Generation is redefining the meaning of gender." *Time Magazine*: March 27, 2017.

tolerance, acceptance, and young people who feel they are transgender. The article goes on to say that, "Hyper-individual, you-do-you young people from across the U.S. are upending the convention that there are only two options for each: male or formal, gay or straight." [2]

This is a difficult conversation and a relatively new one, especially for those from older generations who find differences in gender and sexuality than that assigned at birth as troublesome and confusing. Randall also struggles with this aspect of his father's life, and *This Is Us* accurately depicts the emotional and psychological difficulties family members go through after having to deal with a family member who is struggling with a similar situation.

William and Rebecca: Separate or Similar?

William and Rebecca shared more in common than previously thought. William believed he was completely separate from Jack and Rebecca. They just happened to be Randall's adoptive parents. But a part of Rebecca's past included William as well as music.

In the Memphis episode, William gave up his dream of making it in the music world, dragging his cousin Ricky down with him. He promised to return with sixty new songs after he cares for his mother who is ill. However, he is derailed as he seeks to numb the pain of watching his mother pass away. His girlfriend's flippant use of drugs

---

[2] ibid.

with some friends is more tempting than he can bear, and he turns to drugs to be with her and to anesthetize the ache in his soul. While high, they conceive Randall, rendering him an unfit parent. As he seeks to make peace with Ricky, he tells him how sorry he is for not coming through on his promise to write more songs so he could make it in the music world. Another broken promise, another regret.

Rebecca has this same broken promise. But she did the opposite. She gave up her music career to rear her kids.

Both characters seek to rekindle a lost passion, both desiring to let life stop getting in the way of what's really important to them.

I wonder how much the prodigal son wanted to rekindle a lost passion. Whether it's having a sexual relationship with every woman in the world or drinking to numb the pain of life, we all have a hole in the soul that can only be filled by the love of the Heavenly Father.

William never had the love of his own father, having lost him so early. Losing the only parent he had ever known must have been painful for him.

Rebecca did have two parents as she grew up, although it was far from the Norman Rockwell family picture we have ingrained in our heads. Although short-lived, we know music is important to Rebecca, so much that she's willing to leave her family for a little while to pursue it. We do get a glimpse of Rebecca's longing to reclaim her passion as she tries to go with her old band touring bars and clubs.

Although she went to see William after she and Jack picked up Randall from the hospital, she didn't know much about William. We only know about the book of poems William gives Rebecca, sparking the inspiration to change Randall's name from Kyle. Perhaps William sparked a bit more inspiration in her because we know she gave up on the career altogether after receiving a rejection letter from a record producer regarding her demo. To see her pursue the career after so many years must have taken great courage. It also took great courage for William to stroll into that bar knowing he had disappointed Ricky and the band members. To relive that pain of a shattered dream took him great courage too.

The prodigal son was similar to his brother, too, only they just didn't know it. They both were lost—the younger brother wanting to let his heart go wild, breaking free from all the responsibilities and restrictions a loving father places on his children. But the older son had the gift of his father there with him all the time; yet, he refused to bask in it. He wallowed in what he doesn't have instead of relishing in what he did have. Both needed and wanted an intimate relationship with someone who loved, knew, and accepted them as they were, but only one of them took it. The other had the same invitation extended to him. However, we just don't know if he ever took it.

The prodigal son already had love but turned to wild living, hoping to find a greater love that he soon found didn't exist. In comparison, William wanted love so badly he turned to drugs to numb his pain.

Orphaned like Randall

Although this is not revealed until he dies, William's father died when William was just a baby. He never knew what it was like to have a father play catch with him outside or show him how to ride his bike. He had a loving mother whom raised and cared for him the best she could. But the God-shaped hole that results from sons who need their dads at a certain age became impossible for his mother to fill.

Randall on the other hand, had a father who cared for him as if he was his own

father. Doing push-ups while Randall is on his back, Jack promises to do everything in his power to rear Randall to be a good man. However, Randall is orphaned like William, but in a different way. No matter how much Jack loves him and does his best with him, Randall's deep-seated need to find his real father trumps his loving relationship with his adopted dad.

Although we don't know how long Randall has been searching for his dad, we do know he has been searching, even hiring a private investigator to assist him. What becomes a one-time encounter turns into a loving gesture of grace and hospitality as Randall invites William to live with him once he finds out his dad has cancer. Randall's yearning for a dad is now found again, if only for a short time, which is why William's departure from the show so early is a bit of a shock for us as viewers.

We wanted Randall and William to continue cranking up the music and rolling the window down. We wanted them to play catch so William could experience what his father's love is really like. We wanted them to take that trip to Memphis because it's the one memory they have of just the two of them, and it's William's opportunity to let Randall into his world: a world filled with piano bars, music, and ducks.

The scene where Randall cries at the ducks who pass by his car after he's on his way home from Memphis after his father's passing is so poignant. It wasn't just that Randall finally got a chance to see the ducks his father wanted him to see. The scene is of a mother leading her babies into an unknown world as they cross the street. That's the moment where Randall realizes he's alone. We weep along with him as he discovers this insight and has to go home and tell his wife and kids his news. No child wants to bury his parent. But Randall has had to do this twice, and it's a part of Randall's character that makes us as viewers love him more and more.

Of course, nothing prepares us for the last scene as William prepares to die in the hospital. Randall, normally the anxious one, maintains perfect composure as he holds

William's head in his hands, takes deep breaths with him and tells him to "just breathe," mimicking the tactics Jack took to calm Randall down from his anxiety when he was a boy. The beauty of William's last breaths play out as William dreams of meeting his mother in heaven and relishes in his last moments with his son.

"My boy," is one of the last words he says to Randall. And in that moment, Randall has gotten the acknowledgment and approval from his father he has been looking for his whole life.

Randall, using the same technique his father used with him whenever he was anxious, places both his hands on William's face and says, "Just breathe." Together they take William's last breath together, and Randall is left orphaned once again.

A tearjerker for viewers with Randall's need for love and approval finally met, he can finally move on knowing he finally got to meet the father he never knew. The pain of having to lose a father twice is not lost on us as an audience either, knowing that Jack passed away when Randall was a teen. Orphaned yet again, Randall has to now cope with the pain of losing a father for the second time. Only this time, William's influence on him remains. Now donning William's hat at his celebration party, Randall says, "He changed me."

Because of William, we are changed, too. And we are better people because of him.

I'm team Kate ₄-Evah.

Toby

Chapter Sixteen
Toby and the Modern-Day Jeremiah

No matter who you are, everyone loves Toby. From his proclamation of "Team Kate 4Evah" to Rebecca when she tried to triangulate him into her tension-filled relationship with Kate to his over-the-top proposal where each shirt he removed spelled out "Will you marry me?", everyone would love to have a Toby in their lives. He's the best cheerleader, he loves Kate unconditionally, and he comes with no strings attached (unless you count his heart attack and unpredictable bouts with depression, of course.)

Although I love his character, not everyone is convinced of his genuineness. Emma Dibdin, writer of an article in "Cosmopolitan Magazine", "Toby is a Bad Boyfriend on *This Is Us*," says, "Through the first half of season one, I'm legitimately amazed that we're meant to be rooting for this guy as Kate's love bombs Kate into believing he's everything she wants. He comes on way too strong, and tries way too hard, and while those traits can sometimes be endearing, here they come off as borderline controlling."

She continues, "This is Toby's thing. He imposes his agenda on Kate, then plays the nice guy. He does all these "nice things" (his phrase, by the way, and he uses it a lot) for her, pulls out these showy grand gestures, then gets sulky when she doesn't do what he wants in return. He reminds me of a guy I dated once, who planned out a way-too-elaborate second date and then spent all night reminding me how great it was, and how much effort he'd put into planning it, and how nice it would be if I came back to his place at the end of the night. We've all known a guy or five like Toby." [2]

Despite his flaws and insecurities that he carries after being dumped by his wife, he has stuck by Kate's side no matter how badly she treats him (and there are moments when she projects her problems onto him and he blindly picks up the pieces.) This quality almost makes up for his need for affirmation all the time. Although Kate and Toby's relationship may be a bit dysfunctional, they are good for each other in that they both are trying to fill the voids in their lives from people who have rejected them.

In a special episode dedicated to Kate, we meet her as a young twenty-year-old working as a waitress trying to save money to go to college when she meets a customer who takes an interest in her. We soon realize she has slept with him then afterward declares, "You're married, aren't you?" Since we know she's still struggling with the loss of her father, she lowers herself to become intimate with a married man simply because he showed an interest in her.

The best display of love is Toby's supportive nature when Kate loses their baby. Kate shuts him out initially because she thinks he can't possibly relate to what she's

[2] Dibdin, Emma. "Toby is a Bad Boyfriend on This Is Us." *Cosmopolitan Magazine* (accessed October 3, 2017) http://bit.ly/2DYeMV8

going through. But in his grief, he still thinks about Kate's feelings.

Before the miscarriage, Kate ordered a bathtub for the baby, which is scheduled to be delivered the day when the miscarriage takes place. Toby drives to the package delivery facility and tracks down the package to intercept it so Kate doesn't have to see it. This behavior is typical of Toby's grand gestures, but this time he doesn't do it out of a need to be affirmed but rather out of love and support for Kate.

Previously, Toby filled the void in his life with food (as did Kate.) After he got divorced, he had his first bout of depression that left him immobilized in bed. Now that they've found each other, they've filled that void for love and acceptance that food had provided.

What we love about Toby is not just his romantic gestures and witty personality but also that he is willing to see Kate through her struggles despite his own feelings. Similar to Jeremiah, the weeping prophet, Toby receives rejection by most people around him.

Rejection is Their Common Bond

Not much has been revealed about Toby until now, but in the Las Vegas episode, we finally learn something about Toby. Toby has a younger brother! We also know that he and his brother are far apart in age (ten years), which has placed a permanent wedge between their relationship.

Toby, disclosing his inner nerd and penchant for the "Dungeons and Dragons" game, tells Randall and Kevin, "It's sad to hear your six-year-old brother tell you, 'I don't want to play with you anymore,' and he means it!"

If I didn't love Toby enough already, he has given yet another reason to love him more! It's obvious Randall and Kevin are not excited about hanging out with him, but Toby reveals they are his only friends. He then says his brother rejected him when he was a teen because Toby was a nerd.

We learn that Toby's parents are divorced and have spent more time fighting over alimony payments than spending time with their son. It's also obvious in their exchange the day of his wedding that they don't approve of Kate and her treatment of him, but Toby wants none of it. He doesn't trust their advice because of their lack of presence in his life up until now.

The prophet Jeremiah in the Bible also knows the pain of being rejected by those around him, but for a different reason: "You deceived me, LORD, and I was deceived; you overpowered me and prevailed. I am ridiculed all day long; everyone mocks me. Whenever I speak, I cry out proclaiming violence and destruction. So the word of the LORD has brought me insult and reproach all day long. But if I say, 'I will not mention his word or

212

speak anymore in his name,' his word is in my heart like a fire, a fire shut up in my bones. I am weary of holding it in; indeed, I cannot" (Jeremiah 20: 7-9.)

From the beginning of his life, the Lord has called Jeremiah to become His mouthpiece. But Jeremiah is anything but confident: "Ah, Sovereign Lord," I said, "I do not know how to speak, I am only a child." Jeremiah, unsure of his ability is similar to Toby in that Toby loves Kate, but he brings the baggage he carries from his past marriage into the relationship. Jealous of her and Kevin's relationship and wondering if he is enough for her, he doubts if he can be the man she's looking for in her life.

As Jeremiah was called to speak the Word of the Lord, Toby is also a mouthpiece in Kate's life, too, often encouraging her when she gets too down on herself:

> "I can live without pizza and cookies and potato chips and whatever that brownie thing was that they were serving on the plane. The one thing I cannot live without is you."

Toby has his flaws just like Jack...or Kevin...or Randall...or anyone else. I'm one viewer who hopes the new episodes dive more into his backstory in the seasons to come. But one thing is for certain: He loves Kate. We love him for that too.

You and me? We can do anything.

Beth

Chapter Seventeen
Beth and the Modern-Day Priscilla

Not much has been revealed about Beth, Randall's strong yet passionate counterpart. From his mother to Yvette (the woman from the pool), strong women surround his life. But this book, much like Randall, would not be the same without mentioning her. Protective of her husband's fragile mental state, willing to ask bold yet necessary questions to William, and opening her home to an initial stranger, Beth makes Randall and everyone's life better just by her presence. Beth feels deeply, and audiences feel deeply with her in return. She's a great mother, helping to rear two independent, beautiful daughters. She works to contribute to the family income. Although she may seem ordinary, Randall is a better person because of her. Because of her support, Randall is empowered to change the world.

Author Malcolm Venable, in a "TV Guide" piece, writes:

> *"This Is Us* has no shortage of cute couples: Kate (Chrissy Metz) and Dad-joke aficionado Toby (Chris Sullivan); divorced-but-probably-reconciling Kevin (Justin Hartley) and Sophie (Alexandra Breckenridge); even Jack (Milo Ventimiglia) and Rebecca when they're not screaming at each other. But no couple on NBC's time-bending, pop-culture obsessed tearjerker is more adorable than Randall (Sterling K. Brown) and Beth (Susan Kelechi

Watson). The most stable, fun and funny duo on the show, they handled serious curveballs including his anxiety attacks and father's death with smooth, admirable grace."[1]

Beth most reminds me of Priscilla in the Bible, Paul's supporter and Aquila's wife first encountered in Acts and then mentioned in Romans. Although not much is mentioned about Priscilla, what the Bible does say demonstrates she had a huge impact on Paul's life. This is what the Bible says about Priscilla:

> "After this, Paul left Athens and went to Corinth. There he met a Jew named Aquila, a native of Pontus, who had recently come from Italy with his wife Priscilla, because Claudius had ordered all Jews to leave Rome. Paul went to see them, and because he was a tentmaker as they were, he stayed and worked with them" (Acts 18: 2-3).

We see her again later in the same chapter:

> "When Apollos wanted to go to Achaia, the brothers and sisters encouraged him and wrote to the disciples there to welcome him. When he arrived, he was a great help to those who by grace had believed" (Acts 18:25-27).

---

[1] Venable, Malcolm. "This Is Us: 7 Times Randall and Beth Gave Us Relationship Goals" TVGuide.com http://bit.ly/2IFDGb5

In his blog post "Seven of My Favorite women of the Bible," blogger Jack Wellman encapsulates why Priscilla, wife of Aquila, was a pillar of the early church in Jerusalem:

> "Aquila and Priscilla were both tentmakers as was Paul (Acts 18:1-3) and went on Paul's missionary trip to Syria (Acts 18:18). Paul must have known that they would be useful in proclaiming the gospel with him and so they accompanied him. They knew the gospel well for when they heard Apollos of Alexandria teaching out of the Scriptures (the Old Testament) about Christ they informed him of more than just John's baptism. Afterwards, he became an even greater evangelist for the early church (Acts 18:25-28). Paul clearly knew the value of these two believers as he called them, "my fellow workers in Christ Jesus, who risked their necks for my life" (Romans 16:3). It's one thing to proclaim the gospel, it is yet another to risk their lives for it, but they did not shrink back from this God-given commission. There is little doubt that they were co-laborers with Paul and were unafraid to point others to eternal life in Christ Jesus even if it meant death."[1]

This female issue might be easy to skip or ignore, but the significance is two-fold. In that biblical society, women were treated as lower than dogs on society's totem

---

[1] Wellman, Jack. "7 of My Favorite Women in the Bible." Patheos.com. http://bit.ly/2QvGBFT

pole. To be mentioned by name means she must have played an integral part in Paul's life. Not only that, but Paul names her as a "supporter in Christ." He attributes his spiritual training to Priscilla and her husband: "Greet Priscilla and Aquila, my co-workers in Christ Jesus" (Romans 16:3).

So many Christians hold Paul in high esteem as a person whose life they want to emulate: sacrificing everything, including their own safety for the sake of spreading the Gospel message. To think that Priscilla had an influence on Paul to be a better evangelist and a better man is such an honoring tribute.

Beth is an ordinary woman too. She is a wife we often see in the background. She doesn't get as many emotional monologues as Kevin, Kate, or Randall, so she's easy to forget. But her mere presence in Randall's life makes him a better man.

Priscilla couldn't do the work of shaping Paul's life without Aquila, her husband. Beth can't do the work of shaping William and her children's lives without Randall. Together they're a team.

The audience's first glimpse of Beth is when she and Randall have taken their girls to their sports activities that have two games going on at the same time. Beth looks on as she watches her one child pushing other girls down in an attempt to score a goal.   Randall watches as his other daughter, who takes more interest in braiding her friend's hair than in her game. "Switch," Randall says, and the two-change direction to watch the other child's game.

I love the first impression we get of Beth. She's a helpmate to Randall yet is not held back by him in any way. It's obvious Randall is able to pass on the example that Rebecca and Jack had set for him to be the best he could be growing up and to set high goals and work to achieve them.

Although not much is mentioned about Beth's profession, we do know she works and is respected at her job. She's Randall's counterpart, taking on the main role of caregiver in the home when Randall has his nervous breakdown as well as asking William the hard questions like "Are you really sick?" upon first meeting him. Once her guard is down, she acquires a great fondness for William (Who doesn't love William?), even baking him "special" brownies to help with the pain of his cancer. Although medicinal marijuana sparks a debate among believers and non-believers, one thing is for sure: Beth has a loose side. And we like it. When Randall returns home from his Memphis trip without his father and Beth hears of his news, she's deeply saddened. Once a man whom she distrusted has now passed, and she never got to say goodbye.

And then the postcard arrives.

Calling her "the daughter he never had," this moment for Beth reveals William loved her as much as he loved his own son and gives Beth the closure she needs.

We're not aware whether Beth's parents are still living, but we do know her mother has fallen, and compassionate and caring Beth runs to her rescue, despite the mounting stress going on in the home.

Beth Tells It Like It Is

Another way Beth reminds me of Priscilla is that Beth's not afraid to speak her mind. Beth awakens and finds Randall unable to sleep. She says, "How long is your once crack addicted biological father going to be staying here?"

What a statement!

Apollos in the Bible, a learned man, speaks boldly to Paul in the synagogue: "When Priscilla and Aquila heard him, they invited him to their home and explained to him the way of God more adequately." Because of Priscilla and Aquila's willingness to speak to the man regarding the gospel, Apollos was able to share what he knew to others: "When Apollos wanted to go to Achaia, the brothers and sisters encouraged him and wrote to the disciples there to welcome him. When he arrived, he was a great help to those who by grace had believed" (Acts 18:27).

I respect strong women (I would describe myself as one). The Bible speaks about many women who took great risks to follow God, even at the expense of their own lives. Esther approached her husband's throne uninvited even though she could have been killed. Because of her boldness, the Jews were spared. Because of Lois's and Eunice's dedication to the faith, Timothy is a man worthy of Paul's mentorship. The woman at the well, initially hesitant to be seen in public due to her sin, is bold enough to tell people, "He told me everything I ever did." Who can forget the virgin Mary who sacrificed public ridicule and humiliation as well as Joseph's favor because she was willing to accept God's invitation to be Jesus' mother? Just as *This Is Us* wouldn't be the same without Beth, the Bible wouldn't be the same without strong women who are willing to let God use them to accomplish His purposes.

Strong but Loving

In season two, we get an intimate glance into Beth's life. All along, Beth is portrayed as a strong woman who keeps Randall's family intact. However, we see the toll that being the strong one takes on her when she's thrust into a role I'm not sure she ever wanted in the first place.

Randall's gesture of giving her candy and a note that said, "You're all heart," reveals that Beth has just as big (if not bigger) a heart as Randall. After all, who opens her heart and home to a complete stranger? To be a foster mom is one of the hardest jobs in the world. Only a strong woman could be up for the challenge.

In the season two finale, we discover that Beth isn't a stranger to being a foster caretaker when we meet her cousin whom she and her mom took in as a child. Beth already understands the up and downs of opening her home to a stranger; thus, her willingness to share her gift of hospitality with others enriches the lives of those around her.

Beth's biblical counterpart, Priscilla, demonstrates her gift of hospitality too: "The churches in the province of Asia send you greetings. Aquila and Priscilla greet you warmly in the Lord, and so does the church that meets at their house" (1 Corinthians 16:19). Because Beth has taken in children before, she's the perfect person to take in Deja and other kids like her. In fact, Beth's such a great example of caring for the downtrodden, her daughter chooses to work in the foster care system when she grows up. What an example! People may view Beth as being tough, but she has just enough caring and love in her heart to change the world.

Beth is my favorite character, and for good reason. I hope Fogelman and crew give her character the proper development it deserves.

Chapter Eighteen
Testimonies

When I first saw the commercials highlighting the premiere of the show, to me it looked like any other new drama.

When it premiered on September 20, 2016, I watched just to see what it was like. I soon discovered *This Is Us* was not like any other new drama:

- The twist at the end captivated me when realizing the storylines of Kate, Kevin, and Randall are that of three siblings.

- Jack and Rebecca, who are about to give birth to triplets, are actually the married couple years later.

- I was watching the effects of Jack's and Rebecca's decisions in the 80s and 90s, which have affected them as adults.

Yes, I was hooked.

The storytelling was superb, the acting top notch, and the storylines provided a unique perspective on the issues plaguing people today. Also, the blurring of the program's storylines and mixing of timelines appeared eerily similar to the storytelling style of *Lost*, another show with blatant Christian overtones. Little did I know (or NBC, for that matter) that this production wouldn't just be another television show. It would become, at least for me, a phenomenon.

I am convinced this show will raise the bar on how television stories are told, and in twenty years we might look back and say this show changed television.

As I watch interviews with the cast members about how the show has changed their lives, many of the cast members are overcome with emotion of how lucky they feel to be a part of this artistic masterpiece.

The stories of how many people's lives have been changed by this show are amazing. I want to take a moment to share some of those stories here, both from printed articles in the media and personal stories of people I know who have shared testimonies with me about their experience with this show as well.

Tweets from Twitter

#ThisIsUs doesn't have commercials, they have emotional reprieve for viewers to recover between scenes.

#EveryoneCries Always hydrate for tomorrow. Whether it's for a workout or an episode of #ThisIsUs.

For me, this show has given me a glimpse into the minds and hearts of the world around me. Not only can I relate to Randall losing a parent—I lost a parent when I was twenty-five—but I also can relate to Kate's struggles with everyone snickering behind her back as an overweight woman dancing with her boyfriend. I can relate to Kevin as he struggles with the meaning of this life and wanting more than just meaningless wealth, fame, and relationships. I understand what it's like to be bullied at school for being different.

Of all the characters on the show, I relate to Rebecca the most. I know what it's like to feel as though you're giving up so much of your dreams and talents to rear children. I loved being a mother to my kids, but there were definitely moments when I felt like I wanted to do more with my life than "just be a mom."

While I worked a low paying job I hated and tried to make ends meet while caring for toddlers, I often fantasized about doing something for myself that allowed me to use my gifts and talents. I dreamed of working in ministry or volunteering in a place where my work would be valued and appreciated, all while changing endless amounts of smelly diapers and looking at the piles of unfolded laundry on the couch.

Rebecca understands this frustration. She's finally getting to pursue her dream of being a singer after many years of being a stay-at-home mom. When Jack barges in backstage before the first show and punches out the piano player, I clenched my teeth and gave Jack looks of disgust as he tried to explain his rage away.

Jack and Rebecca's huge season finale fight was not shocking to me as I have muttered Rebecca's words to myself on many occasions. Many stay-at-home moms who either struggle with staying at home or working outside the home and missing out on the big moments with her kids can understand Rebecca's tension. The show resonates with so many people because the characters speak and feel thoughts and ideas we all have thought at one time or another but just didn't have the courage to say them out loud.

I'm not the only one who has felt a kinship to the show. When I posed three questions to my Facebook friends and family, the following is what I received as responses.

I asked:

1. What do you love most about the show and why?

2. Have you learned anything about yourself or others from watching the show?

3. Which character do you relate to the most and why?

Some answers I received are:

1. "I love the bond between siblings. I learned that even put-together successful people can suffer

from anxiety. I relate most to Rebecca from the flashbacks because I feel sometimes I have lost my identity in parenthood. Not that I have regrets; I just put myself on the back burner too often." Michelle S. Southington, CT

2. "I love that they don't sugarcoat the issues or problems they face. I've learned that if you ask for help, more than likely you'll get it. I relate the most to Randall. I have high expectations of myself like he does for his life, career, etc. But from his experiences I see that not everything is perfect nor should it be." Stephanie P. Wallingford, CT

3. "I love that they kept it real and placed forgiveness and redemption as part of the journey. I learned that as a mother of young-to-adult children, all the effort put into parenting matters—mothers may not be perfect, or be understood by their children, but the love that is there can bring them through the most difficult of situations and is a beautiful example of how people grow together as a family unit. I relate to Randall's wife Beth—trying to keep everything together, being the peacemaker." Pamela H. Granite Falls, NC

4. "I love that the show tells the story of how everyone that crosses our path plays a role and has a purpose in our lives. I believe that God

places us where he needs us to be and with the people we need to be with at the perfect moment. It is up to us to see and appreciate that. This show has made me analyze places and people in my past. I learned that each place, each person shaped who I am today. There are a lot of lessons to be learned from the show. As a viewer, I can't help to be sad for Randall and the lack of time he had with his biological father. As a mother, I understand why Rebecca felt like she was keeping him safe by keeping his biological father from him. We make hard choices as parents. I relate a lot to Rebecca in the sense that as a mother, your passions get set aside so that you can care for your children and husband. I think a lot of us do that. The characters are real. That is what I love the most!" Jami M. Shelton, CT

Although these examples may seem like trivial ways in which a TV show can change lives, there are more dramatic examples. In an article titled "To My Transracial Family, *This Is Us* Is So Much More Than a TV Show," author Rachel Garlinghouse writes:

This Is Us doesn't just tell a story. It tells my family's story. More than eight years ago, my husband and I were painting our kitchen when his cell phone rang. He didn't recognize the number but picked up anyway. His eyes grew wide and he thrust the phone into my hands. It was our adoption agency's new social worker.

We were parents.

When we met our daughter, our whole world changed. She became our everything. And just like Jack and Rebecca, we were two white parents with a black child, which meant that although she was fully our "own" and "real" daughter, we would face obstacles dealing with race that we had absolutely no experience with. Parenting four children who came to us through adoption has been an ongoing lesson in humility, empathy, strength, and change. We have learned, just as Rebecca and Jack did, that love is not enough. Children of color who were adopted by white parents require racial role models and parental knowledge of hair and skin care. Adoptees (people who were adopted) may have a natural desire to know where and who they came from. Biological connections matter, just as Randall demonstrates when he reconnects with his birth father. Just like Jack and Rebecca, our children sometimes face stares or snide comments from strangers as soon as our family enters a room. We too can't help but wince when—once again—our children are asked if they are "real" siblings, or I'm labeled as their "adoptive" mother instead of just their mother...."[1]

---

[1] Garlinghouse, Rachael. "To My Transracial Family 'This is Us' Is So Much More Than Just a TV Show." Babble.com. http://bit.ly/2xYvMoY

Fans of the show feel a sense of connectedness to the characters in a way rarely (if ever0 seen on television. The situations are so real and the characters so down to earth, it's easy to forget it's just a story being played out before our eyes. Instead, it's much easier to believe the characters are our friends and neighbors next door, the mother in the carpool lane, or the person sitting in the pew next to us at church.

Garlinghouse continues:

> "Like the moment we see Rebecca in a flashback, newly home from the hospital with her three little bundles. Cradling Kate and Kevin one by one, she nurses them naturally, but struggles to do the same with Randall. The way she attempts to physically connect with her son symbolizes the deep importance a mother often feels while bonding with her child after an adoption. Making a child one's own can be a struggle for many families who adopt, as each person tries desperately to figure out what belonging, acceptance, and true love means. In so many ways, *This Is Us* perfectly explores the intricate dance that families like mine often encounter. Whether it's the child who deserves to hear truth, the family who seeks to settle into their new "normal," or the biological parent who craves connection and closure, *This Is Us* gets

me emotional every single episode. And I know I'm not alone."[2]

My prayer is that you not read this book and feel like you need to live up to an unrealistic standard. Rather, I hope you see that the characters in the Bible and the characters in the TV show have their place in the greater story that is life—a life interwoven with ups and downs, highs and lows, and a God that is Lord of it all.

Maybe Kevin is right. Maybe life is like a painting and every color makes the tapestry of life. Each of us works on a part of the painting, and when it's complete, it colors our world.

May we follow the example of the Pearson family and allow all the trials and tribulations to make us stronger, to face life with integrity and courage, and to let all of it help us grow closer as a family through it all.

The family that is us.

---

[2] ibid.

About the Author

 Michelle S. Lazurek, pop culture junkie and writer and reviewer for *Movieguide Magazine,* desires to help Christians interact with the world around them in a biblical way, including their TV sets.

She is an award-winning author, speaker, pastor's wife and mother. Winner of the Golden Scroll Children's Book of the Year, the Enduring Light Silver Medal and the Maxwell Award, she is a member of the Christian Author's Network and the Advanced Writers and Speakers Association. She is also an associate literary agent with Wordwise Media Services.

When not occupied with literary pursuits, you can find her sipping a hot latte at Starbucks, reading a good book, or collecting records from the 1980s and 90s. She lives in Pennsylvania with her husband, two children and their crazy dog, Cookie. To purchase the book, please visit her website at www.michellelazurek.com.

More from Michelle Lazurek

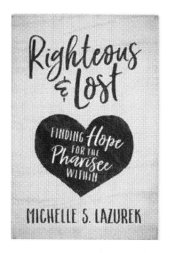

Christians often become burned out on church but don't know why. We can easily become the older brother grumbling in the field, jealous and envious of all the spoils our younger brother receives. This parable is one of longing, of wanting, and of a Father who extends his hand and gives freely to both sons--yet only one gratefully receives. This book will help you identify the attitudes and behaviors hindering you from the intimate walk with God you desire. In *Righteous and Lost*, you will:

~ Explore biblical passages that will help you embrace the love of your Father
~ Identify symptoms of a religious spirit
~ Analyze how a religious spirit can block you from a relationship with God
~ Apply practical tips and advice to prevent a religious spirit from coming back into your life

Available at michellelazurek.com liveway.com, barnesandnoble.com, and Christianbook.com

Made in the USA
Columbia, SC
04 November 2018